LOST
CAR COMPANIES
OF DETROIT

ALAN NALDRETT

THE
History
PRESS

Published by The History Press
Charleston, SC
www.historypress.net

Copyright © 2016 by Alan Naldrett
All rights reserved

First published 2016

ISBN 978.1.5402.0285.7

Library of Congress Control Number: 2015954755

This book is dedicated to those unsung auto pioneers who weren't part of the Big Three automakers. Roy Chapin, Harold Wills, Joe Frazer and many others depicted within these pages who played substantial roles in creating the automobiles of today.

CONTENTS

ACKNOWLEDGEMENTS

I would like to thank my friend Keith Marcero, who got me interested in cars at a time when I thought comic books were way more exciting. Thanks to the many people who provided information or pointed the way toward information, including Bette Carrothers, Kent Cole, Leigh Cole, Eric Gala, Rich Gonyeau, Frank and Sherrel Hissong, Dave Keck, Marty Krist, Bob and Geri Mack, Phyllis and Chuck Maddix, Jammie Naldrett, Ron and Norma Naldrett, Craig Neinhaus, Bob and Laverne Nett, Ruth Presutti, Paul Torney, Gail Zabowski, Ron Bluhm of the Ypsilanti Automotive Heritage Museum and Romie Minor of the National Automotive History Collection of the Detroit Public Library. Thanks to Lynn Keck Lyon, who shot pictures, transported me in her automobile to many car museums and long-lost auto factories, proofread and gave me many good ideas while writing this book. Thanks also to Sally, Lynn's GPS device, who helped us find all those retired auto factories. I'd also like to give many thanks to Dave Castle, who edited the manuscript into legible reading material and made many major contributions and suggestions.

INTRODUCTION

The first motorcar was most likely the steam-powered auto built by Jesuit missionary Ferdinand Verbiest while he was living in China in 1678. It's interesting that a Jesuit minister was the inventor of what parents in the 1950s considered the number one corruptor of morals. The next notable motor-powered vehicle was the 1769 steam vehicle of French army officer Nicolas Cugnot.

By 1801, English inventors Richard Trevithick and Sir Goldsworthy Gurney had built notable "steam carriages." And the battle was on—not only to produce new motorized conveyances but to decide what to call them! At first, "horseless carriage" was often used, especially when many of the early autos were built on buggy frames. As time went on, "motor car" came into prominence as many new car companies used motorcar in their company name. It is spelled as either two words or one word—motorcar. In Latin, auto means itself and mobile means moving. Automobile technically meant "moving by itself." First used in France, the name automobile in the United States is traced most often to an 1897 article in the *New York Times* lamenting the new "automobiles" that had become so popular. That same year, reporter Charlie Shanks wrote about a Winton long-distance trek, calling the vehicle they were traveling in an automobile.

In the United States, Oliver Evans demonstrated a steam carriage in 1805 that worked on land and sea. Steam-powered vehicles were the rage as the Steamer twins, Francis and Freelan, manufactured the Stanley Steamer and other steam vehicles from 1896 all the way up until 1925.

Richard Davenport is credited with building the first working model of an electric car in 1836. By 1900, they were the most popular type of car, at least for women, probably because they were silent, didn't give off noxious fumes and didn't require a crank to start. Even so, all motor-powered vehicles, or "horseless carriages," were not too well regarded in their early days.

In Vermont, an 1896 law required a pedestrian to walk one hundred feet in front of the vehicle to warn anyone who might be in the vicinity. In England, the "Red Flag" law was passed in 1865 stating that a motorcar couldn't go faster than four miles an hour in the country and two miles an hour in the city and that an attendant had to walk ahead of the vehicle with a red flag as a warning to others. This law wasn't repealed until 1896.

Gasoline-powered vehicles were made possible through French inventor Jean Joseph Lenoir's 1863 development of a one-cylinder gas-powered engine. The first to use the engine to power a vehicle was Austrian Siegfried Marcus in 1864. From Germany, Gottlieb Daimler and Karl Benz refined the engineering and began to produce vehicles powered by gasoline. The **Daimler Benz Motor Company** was formed.

In 1884–85, John Clegg and his son, Thomas, built a vehicle known as the Thing and drove it on the streets of Memphis, Michigan. It was a four-seater, powered by a single-cylinder steam engine with a tubular boiler carried in the rear.

The 1893 Benz Velo, short for velocipede, is credited as being the first standard automobile. *Author's collection.*

The Duryea brothers, Charles and Frank, as the **Duryea Motor Wagon Company**, built the first successful commercial gas-powered vehicle in the United States in 1893. They had sold twelve of them by 1896.

In 1896, Charles Brady King's motorcar was the first to be driven on Detroit streets, with Henry Ford following in his own car a few months later. Also in late 1896, Ransom E. Olds drove his first vehicle on the streets of Lansing, Michigan.

The earliest days of the auto industry, starting in the 1890s and before, were referred to as the Veteran Era. Next was the Brass Era, which was from the 1900s to 1915 and was called that because of all the brass used in the early vehicles, usually in the lights or radiators. The next era, from 1915 until 1935, was called the Vintage Era. The short Prewar Era, from 1936 to 1941, ushered in the War Era, which lasted until 1951. The period from 1952 until 1959 was referred to as the Postwar Era, and from 1960 until 1985 was the Classic Era. Everything since 1985 is known as the Modern Era.

By 1900, the U.S. auto industry had been producing vehicles for sale to the general public for barely four years. Steam vehicles comprised about 40 percent of the market, electric vehicles captured 38 percent and gas-powered vehicles brought up the rear at about 22 percent of the market. But both steam and electricity had their drawbacks as fuel for motorcars. Steam cars could take thirty minutes or more for the steam to heat up enough to power the car. Also, riding on top of or alongside the boiler of live steam was dangerous, and many people were scalded to death.

Electric cars had their drawbacks as well. The farthest the best of them could go without a recharge was fifty miles. Running out of power in an area with no electricity was a frequent problem.

Charles Brady King and Henry Ford, along with many other competitors, began producing gasoline-powered motorcars in the 1890s. More than two hundred different companies tried their luck at producing all three types of vehicles, but only a few survived. The companies that lasted bear the names that are the most well-known. They are the "Big Three"—**Ford Motor Company**, **General Motors** and **Chrysler Corporation**.

The founders of these corporate automobile survivors include Henry Ford, who, after driving the second auto down the streets of Detroit, went on to form two unsuccessful auto companies before striking gold with his third, the **Ford Motor Company**. The world headquarters of **Ford** is in Dearborn, Michigan.

General Motors was formed by William "Billy" Durant by absorbing other auto brands, including **Buick** and **Chevrolet**, and was the largest company in the world for many years and remains one of the largest. Its world headquarters is in Detroit.

Chrysler Corporation, formerly owned by **Daimler** and acquired by **Fiat** in 2009, was first formed by Walter Chrysler in 1925 and is the third of the Big Three Detroit corporations.

The stories of the independent auto companies intermingle through the stories of the Big Three, and as their accounts unfold, so do those of the Big Three. These stories take place in states and cities around Detroit that are pieces of the puzzle explaining how Detroit came to be the Motor City.

Many innovations having to do with auto history originated in Detroit. One was the first mile of paved road, which was on Woodward Avenue, between Six and Seven Mile Roads, at the site of Ford's Highland Park Model T plant.

The first stoplight was at Woodward Avenue and Davison Road, which later became the site of the first urban freeway. It took one day to figure out that the bus stops they had built into the Davison Expressway weren't going to work on a freeway.

The railroad industry had developed the system of using red lights to indicate stop, yellow for caution and green for go in the 1830s. In 1920, a Detroit policeman, William L. Potts, invented a traffic light using these colors to direct the growing numbers of autos on the city streets. The Potts design is still used today, with the red light on top and green on the bottom.

It helps to know some of the lingo and definitions that the auto industry developed. The Society of Automobile Engineers (now SAE International) was established in the early 1900s to standardize definitions and engineering concepts. It decided that a "touring car" was "an open car seating four or more with direct entrance to tonneau (the back seat)." A touring car has also been defined as an open car seating five or more. Tonneau could also mean a cover, either hard or soft, used to protect unoccupied passenger seats in a convertible or roadster, or a tonneau could refer to the cargo bed in a pickup truck.

Now, if tonneau seems like a confusing word with way too many definitions, the tonneaux (with an x at the end) was a little different—it was a compartment or rear part of an automobile body containing seats for passengers.

The definition of a coupe was "a closed two-door car body style with a permanently attached fixed roof" or "a four-wheeled enclosed carriage for two passengers and a driver." A roadster was defined as "an open car seating two or three. It may have additional seats on running boards or a rear deck." Additional seating in the rear was called a "rumble seat" or a "dickey seat."

A "cyclecar" was a small, two-passenger, lightweight and inexpensive car, built with basic materials and usually conceived as something between a motorcycle and an auto. Steering was usually by a tiller, which in some cases was in the back seat.

"Brougham" was originally the term for a light, four-wheeled, horse-drawn carriage. The term was adopted for autos built in the carriage style. This style was where the term "horseless carriage" came from, and it was also referred to as a "highwheeler."

Motors or engines used in the early cars were often referred to by their brand names. For example, a "Continental" was an engine made by the **Continental Motors Company**, and a "Lycoming" was a product of the **Lacombe Company**. "Marque" and "nameplate" are two different terms to designate a brand name of an automobile. It would often designate a division of auto within an auto company, such as **Hudson**'s Essex and Terraplane. The "badge" was a metal plate with the logo of the company that went on the front grille.

Great Britain had many terms different from the United States. Here are some of the main ones:

- bonnet—the hood of a car
- boot—the trunk of a car
- coupe de ville—town car
- estate car or shooting brake—a station wagon
- gearbox—transmission
- mudguard or wing—fender
- petrol—gasoline
- saloon—sedan
- sedanca de ville—town car
- silencer—muffler
- track—tread
- two-stroke—two-cylinder
- windscreen—windshield

There were a multitude of U.S. car companies, especially in the Midwest. While the majority of these companies didn't survive, there were quite a few that had many prosperous years. Several companies existed only on paper (and in dreams) and never assembled a single car. Companies were formed that produced a single prototype and then took it to the Chicago, Detroit or New York Auto Show to see if they could get anyone interested in buying or producing them. Companies as diverse as **Sears and Roebuck**, **International Harvester** and **Briggs and Stratton** all tried their hand at auto manufacturing. Most were never heard from again.

Most of the early auto companies failed, many because of inefficient assembly procedures, questionable management and business practices and bad marketing decisions, such as making luxury cars in a market already glutted with luxury cars. Nowadays, classic cars whose parent company has folded are called orphan cars. Each company had unique stories, but even if this book had unlimited pages, it would still be hard to chronicle them all.

The Big Three companies have many books written about them detailing their founders, their company histories and their contributions to the auto industry. But there were more than two hundred companies that folded and left scant records—companies that made important discoveries, introduced important innovations and helped move the auto industry forward to what it is today.

1

OLDS MOTOR WORKS BECOMES THE FIRST CAR COMPANY

After the initial shock of seeing a self-propelled motor conveyance, many people began to ponder owning one. For some, the pondering led to wanting to build automobiles and sell them to the public. A few were driven by the thought of big money, and others were just mechanically motivated and wanted to build superior motor conveyances.

Successful businessmen from many different professions began to have a sideline in automobile manufacturing. Many were originally carriage and buggy builders or bicycle shop owners. Appliance factory owners made springs, wheels and other parts for automobile production before producing a complete vehicle themselves. The manufacturers of the luxury auto **Pierce-Arrow** started off making birdcages.

The next step after inventing a new type of motor conveyance was manufacturing it and marketing it to the public. Probably the biggest obstacle to the production of autos in the United States was the Selden Patent. After George Brayton constructed a two-cycle combustion engine with a single cylinder that burned gasoline for fuel, he patented it with the U.S. Patent Office in 1872. When Brayton exhibited his engine at the Philadelphia Centennial Fair in 1876, he caught the eye of attorney George Selden. Knowing a good thing when he saw it, Selden bought the patent from Brayton. The Selden Patent essentially became a patent on the automobile, and all automakers were required to pay royalties to Selden. Finally, Henry Ford challenged the patent in court and won, successfully arguing that the **Ford** four-cylinder engine was not covered under the patent. This also freed other companies from having to pay royalties to manufacture autos, as most had a two-cylinder engine or higher, and the auto patent was no longer pursued after the Ford case.

Ransom E. Olds Builds a Steam Motorcar and an Auto Empire

The rise of the Detroit motorcar started in 1897 with the formation of the **Olds Motor Vehicle Company**. **Olds** was the first auto company incorporated in the United States. Its history could be said to have started ten years before in 1887 when Ransom E. Olds (1864–1940) built a cumbersome, three-wheeled, steam-driven vehicle. The vehicle he built in 1891 ran better and was the subject of a *Scientific American* article.

By 1896, Ransom Olds had developed a gasoline-powered vehicle with a five-horsepower, single-cylinder engine. Olds formed a company to produce his vehicle, but only a few of the 1898 models were produced because his subsidiary, the **Olds Gasoline Engine Works**, was so busy producing engines for the other inventors trying to develop new motor vehicle companies.

In 1899, the **Olds Motor Works** was formed, combining Olds's two previous companies and capitalizing the new company to mass produce motorcars. With lumber baron Samuel Latta Smith providing capital (under the provision that his sons Frederick and Angus be given jobs), Ransom Olds developed many different models, including electrics.

One of Smith's provisions was that production would be in Detroit. The **Olds Motor Works** purchased five acres of land near the island of Belle Isle. The company built a three-story factory at Detroit's Jefferson and Concord Streets in 1900, the first factory in the world to be constructed specifically for auto production. But the factory caught fire, burning all the plans and prototypes except one for the Curved Dash Olds, which was driven out of the blazing factory just in time to save it. In 1901, the Lansing Business Council talked Olds into opening a new factory in Lansing.

Because all the other prototypes were lost in the factory fire, Olds had no other choice but to manufacture the single-cylinder, seven-horsepower, two-speed transmission motorcar called the Curved Dash Oldsmobile. The car cost $650 and was an instant success. Production increased from hundreds to thousands of autos in one year. This was helped by **Olds Motor Works**

Ransom Olds built a Queen Anne–style mansion at 720 South Washington Street in Lansing. In the house's garage, Olds had a turntable installed to turn the car around so he didn't have to back out of the driveway. The house was demolished when the I-496 Expressway was built. Ironically, the new highway was named for Olds. *Courtesy of the Historic American Buildings Survey.*

The **Olds Motor Vehicle Company** factory was located on what is now Martin Luther King Boulevard by the Grand River in downtown Lansing, the original site of the Michigan State Fairgrounds. When the factory was demolished in 2006, it had most recently been a **GM** assembly plant. *Author's collection.*

being the second company to use mass production techniques (the first was the luxury car maker **Winton Company**). These techniques were later expanded upon with assembly lines in Henry Ford's Piquette Plant in the Milwaukee Junction and his Highland Park plant on Woodward Avenue. For its premier years, the Curved Dash Olds, the first car to carry the Oldsmobile name, was the top-selling car in the United States. Its place in pop culture was assured when the Curved Dash Olds became immortalized in the song "In My Merry Oldsmobile."

In 1906, the controlling interest in the **Olds** company was still held by Samuel Latta Smith and his son Fred. The Smiths were not happy with the diminishing sales of the original brand—even though it had been the number two brand in the nation in 1902 and was number one from 1903 to 1905. The Smiths wanted to stop producing the Curved Dash Olds that had proved so popular. Founder and chief inventor Ransom Olds disagreed with this move and quit the company he had started.

Olds went on to manufacture another car with his name, the REO. His name continued to be immortalized in the original Oldsmobile brand until it was discontinued more than one hundred years later, when it was the oldest continuing American brand. When Ransom Eli Olds

The 1902 Olds on the left was called the "Curved Dash" model and was the top-selling car in the United States in 1902 and 1903. Next to it is the 1905 Roadster, which had the engine in the rear and a tool box under the hood. *Author's collection.*

The REO factory in Lansing was used to build the REO Speedwagon and the other popular cars and trucks manufactured by Ransom E. Olds after he left **Olds Motor Works**. *Author's collection.*

left the **Olds Motor Works**, he named his new company for himself, the **R.E. Olds Company**. This did not make the proprietors of his old company very happy, since they had purchased the rights to the Olds name when Ransom Olds left the company. Ransom reasoned that he had not sold them his initials, and the REO Motor Company was born. Ransom Olds's new company was outselling his old company by 1907. That must have made him happy.

With Ransom, the **Olds Motor Works** began to produce alternative styles, including the Palace Touring and the Flying Roadster, which were luxury brands produced from 1906 until 1908. At the tail end of 1908, the company had been losing money while producing fewer autos. The company was purchased by William Durant as a part of his new auto conglomerate, **General Motors (GM)**. As a **GM** company, Oldsmobile continued to lean toward the luxury end of the **GM** vehicle line throughout the rest of its years. In 1942, the **Olds Motor Works** nameplate was changed to **General Motors**, Oldsmobile Division. In 2004, barely after its 100th anniversary, the auto line was retired by **GM**.

From 1905 until 1912, Ransom Olds guided the fortunes of the REO Motor Company. In 1912, he retired to handle other interests. The REO nameplate continued until 1938, as the REO went from being offered in one- and two-cylinder versions to the eight-cylinder limousine versions of the REO in 1931 through 1934. One of the most famous REO models was the REO Speedwagon, which was further immortalized in popular culture as the name of a popular rock band in the 1970s and '80s.

2

THE SHORT REIGN OF STEAM CARS

The first motor vehicles were powered by steam, and the first commercial steam-driven vehicles were produced in the early 1800s in England. In 1883, Sylvester Roper produced a steam-powered vehicle in Boston, Massachusetts. This vehicle made its way to the Henry Ford Museum in Dearborn, where it is the oldest motor vehicle in the collection.

NEW ENGLAND'S EARLY 1900S FAD

Make and Sell a Steam Car

In 1900, as automobiles began to proliferate enough to warrant statistics, the number one selling type of car was the steam car. The early popularity of the steam car was responsible for the increase in short-lived steam car–producing companies in a lot of different areas east of the Mississippi. In fact, Massachusetts could be considered the steam car capital since so many were manufactured there. The most famous was the Stanley Steamer, but there was also the American Steam Car of West Newton; the Ross, which was produced in Newtonville; and the Locomobile of Watertown. Finally, Boston's **Colonial Company** manufactured the Kent's Pacemaker steam auto, and the **Waltham Company** built the American Waltham.

The Steamobile was produced in Keene, New Hampshire, and farther west was **Standard Steam Company** in St. Louis, Missouri. Syracuse, New York, was home to **Century Motor Vehicle** and the **Stearns Steam Carriage Company**, which was founded by Edward C. Stearns. This included the **Keystone** of Lebanon, Pennsylvania, and the **Reading Steamer Company** of Reading, Pennsylvania. In the Midwest, there were more steam car companies, including **American Steamer** of Elgin, Illinois; the **Aultman** of Canton, Ohio; and **Coats Steam Car** of Sandusky, Ohio.

The Hudson Company produced a steam vehicle, the Hudson, named for the city it was produced in—Hudson, Michigan. This is a different Hudson than the company that produced gasoline-powered autos from 1909 through 1957. The **Jackson Motor Company** of Jackson, Michigan, and the **Doble-Detroit Steam Motors Company** of Detroit also manufactured steam cars.

Abner Doble (1890–1861) built his first steam car while he was still in high school. He entered college in 1910. His steam design was considered the most sophisticated up to that time because no steam escaped from his power unit—it all went to power the automobile. For many people, the biggest downside to the steam auto was the amount of time it took to create enough steam to power the car. But the Doble could start in less than a minute and a half, and it could hold twenty-four gallons of water, which would power it for a good 1,500 miles.

The first Doble was available in 1917 and eleven thousand preorders were received, but war priorities cut into this, and only about forty-five were eventually produced. It didn't help that Abner Doble was a perfectionist who had problems producing his cars on such a large scale. The company failed before it could make use of a new factory purchased in Emeryville, California, in 1924.

The Stanley Twins Produce Successful Steam Cars

The most successful and famous steam car was the Stanley Steamer. It was produced by the **Stanley Motor Carriage Company** of Newton, Massachusetts, from 1902 until 1924 and was named for its creators, twin brothers Francis and Freelan Stanley. (An interesting fact regarding car companies is the number of brother teams involved in the manufacturing of

The 1902 Stanley Steamer had the driver in the back with room for two passengers up front. *Author's collection.*

automobiles. These teams include brothers with the last name of Apperson, Briscoe, Dodge, Duryea, Fisher, Graham, Hupp, Packard, Stanley, Studebaker and Welch.)

From 1899 to 1903, the Stanleys created a different version each year. They financed manufacturing their vehicles through the sale of their photographic plate company to the Eastman Kodak Company. In 1898 and 1899, they sold more autos than any other company—more than two hundred. In 1902, they sold their old designs to the **Locomobile Company** and organized the **Stanley Motor Carriage Company** to manufacture a new design.

The Stanley twins continued to improve their autos, moving the steam boiler to the front of the car, adding twin cycle engines and securing the engine better to safeguard the driver. The Stanley Steamer set an auto speed record in 1908—it ran one mile in 28.2 seconds. In fact, the steam-powered auto record set in 1911 wasn't broken until 2009.

The Stanley Steamer continued to be a top-selling car, with more than five hundred units sold in 1907. But by 1910, the efficiency of the internal combustion engine improved. The problematic crank starter, the largest cause of injuries in the early gas-powered cars, gave way to the self-starting engine. Fuel efficiency in the gas-powered engines improved tremendously. The Stanleys fought back by playing on the public's fears that internal combustion engines were "internal explosion engines."

In 1918, Francis Stanley died when he drove his car into a woodpile while trying to avoid farm wagons on the road. His brother, Freelan, sold the company to Prescott Warren. The company staggered on for a while, although no models were produced with a more than twenty horsepower engine. The lower speeds and higher prices of the steam vehicle eventually led to its demise in 1924.

The **Rauch & Lang Carriage Company** started in Cleveland in 1865 and produced some of the most luxurious carriages in the area. Jacob Rauch was a blacksmith and wagon maker, and Charles Lang was a real estate magnate. In 1903, they decided to branch out into automobiles and purchased some remnants of the **Buffalo Electric Carriage Company**, which manufactured electric vehicles called the Buffalo in Buffalo, New York. Lang and Rauch were sales agents for the company until 1905, when they brought out an electric vehicle of their own, the Rauch & Lang Electric. By 1907, they had sold enough vehicles to buy the **Hertner Electric Company**, which had supplied their controllers and motors. The company thereafter produced the whole vehicle in-house.

In 1908, the company was turning out more than five hundred electric cars per year. Everything was progressing nicely until 1911, when it was sued by the **Baker Motor Vehicle Company** for infringing on a patent concerning the mounting of rear springs. All was settled by 1915 when both companies, faced with declining sales, merged and became the **Baker R&L Company**. During 1916–20, the company also built the Owen Magnetic vehicle. The Owen Magnetic wasn't actually a vehicle that ran on a new kind of propulsion, magnetic power, but an expensive and elegant six-cylinder electric vehicle that lasted from 1915 until 1921 and then went into receivership. One of the Owen Magnetic's most notable aspects was an advertising campaign with the slogan "Driving a Melody." Famous tenor Enrico Caruso had an Owen, so maybe the appeal to musicians worked.

Businessman Ray Deering bought out the electric car portion of the company in 1920 and continued producing the car called the Rauch & Lang. In 1922, the company branched out into making gasoline-powered vehicles and taxis. The firm struggled on until the Great Depression. At the time of its demise, it had been working on a hybrid vehicle that could run on both gasoline and electricity.

Not Really Crazy

Manufacturing the Locomobile

The **Locomobile Company of America** started in 1899. It was, at first, one of the most successful steam cars, despite its name—which wasn't meant to indicate that the car was "loco," the Spanish word for crazy, but was a name taken from the words "locomotive" and "automobile."

In its first two years, the company was located in Watertown, Massachusetts, but production was transferred to Bridgeport, Connecticut, in 1900. It manufactured small steam cars with the design it had purchased from the Stanley brothers. The price was right for many people, $600, even though the car had many problems. It was prone to kerosene fires and had very small water tanks that took a long time to raise enough steam to power the car. They weren't really sturdy, were steered with a tiller and were built on bicycle frames and chain-driven. The car was only good for twenty miles before the water would need to be refilled. Nevertheless, more than four thousand were sold between 1899 and 1902. It was the top-selling car in the United States in 1901 and 1902. During the Second Boer War, the Locomobile was the first car to be used in wartime. It was used for its generator and to carry search lights.

The Rauch & Lang Electric Car was a successful auto, selling over five hundred units a year. *Author's collection.*

By 1903, the Stanleys had started their own company with an improved steam car design. The **Locomobile Company** decided to switch to gasoline-powered vehicles and sold back the design to the Stanleys for $20,000 what it had purchased just a few years before for $250,000. The company started to produce luxury-sized autos with gasoline engines in 1904 but kept the Locomobile name, starting with the Locomobile Touring Car. It developed a good reputation for speedy, dependable autos and in 1919 brought out its most remembered marque, the Model 48.

In 1922, Locomobile was purchased by **GM** founder Billy Durant for his new venture, **Durant Motors**. Durant had been ousted by **General Motors** the previous year, and so Durant once again purchased independent companies to form a new conglomerate. The popular Locomobile Model 48 was continued, and another model, called the Model 90, was added. The following year, a smaller vehicle, called the Junior 8, was manufactured. The Locomobile factory also started to produce the low-priced auto the Flint. When **Durant Motors** ended in 1931, so did the Locomobile.

Billy Durant Starts a Few Car Conglomerates

William "Billy" Crapo Durant's first venture was with Josiah Dallas Dort in 1886, establishing the **Flint Road Cart Company** and, later, the **Durant-Dort Carriage Company**. When Billy amicably departed to form **GM**, J.D. Dort carried on with the carriage company. They remained lifelong friends and contributed to each other's ventures.

J.D. Dort eventually succumbed to motorcar fever and formed the **Dort Motor Car Company** in 1915. His chief engineer was Louis Chevrolet, who had met Durant when he was a driver for the **Buick Motor Company**. Together, Chevrolet and famed French designer Etienne Planche designed the Dort, a car admired by all. With their Lycombe engine and reliable reputation, Dorts were around from 1915 until 1924.

The 1915 and 1916 Dort models were both four-cylinder, seventeen-horsepower touring vehicles. The vehicles were so popular that an additional factory was opened in Canada (south of Detroit in Windsor, Ontario). The Canadian branch was managed by William Gray, and the vehicle produced there was called the Gray Dort.

The **Dort Motor Car Company** built cars in Detroit's local rival motor city, Flint. (Flint was known as the "Vehicle City" not for its auto production

The **Durant-Dort Carriage Company** office, built in 1895, is located at 316 West Water Street in Flint. The building was, at first, the headquarters of the carriage company. Later, it was where the **Buick**, **Chevrolet** and **General Motors** companies were organized. *Author's collection.*

Thomas Edison owned a Detroit Electric car and worked with Henry Ford on developing a rechargeable battery for electric cars. The Edison nickel-iron battery became the top choice for electric vehicles. This image is from 1913. *Courtesy of the Smithsonian Institute.*

The **Chevrolet Motor Car Company** was started by Louis Chevrolet in 1911 and featured the overhead-valve, six-cylinder engine he developed. Chevrolet sold his interest in the company to **General Motors** in 1916 and became a full-time race car driver. *Author's collection.*

but for its manufacturing of buggies.) In 1917, the Cloverleaf Roadster was built, as well as two sedan styles (sedans were "closed in" models, as opposed to open model touring vehicles). In 1918, a coupe model was added. Near the end of its production, Dort brought out luxurious vehicles with **Rolls-Royce** styling and names like the Harvard and the Yale. Its peak year was 1920, when Dort sold thirty thousand cars. In 1923, a six-cylinder model was offered. By 1924, J.D. Dort was ready to retire and liquidated the **Dort Motor Car Company**, selling the factory to the **A.C. Spark Plug Company**.

Louis Chevrolet developed an overhead valve, six-cylinder engine in 1909 in his workshop on Grand River Boulevard in Detroit. He then formed the **Chevrolet Motor Company** with William Durant to produce cars with the new engine. Louis Chevrolet sold his interest in the company to William Durant a few years later and went into auto racing. The Chevrolet automobile was to become the **GM** standard bearer.

3

ELECTRIC CARS SHORT CIRCUIT

In the early years of the auto industry, electric cars appeared to have a bright future. Even Henry Ford's wife, Clara, had a Detroit Electric. In fact, the electric car was popular with women because it didn't require turning a hand crank to get the engine running, didn't make a lot of noise and didn't have noxious gasoline odors. Other famous electric car owners included Thomas Edison, Mamie Eisenhower and John D. Rockefeller, who bought two, one for his wife and one for himself.

Electric cars got their start in Scotland in 1837. William Morrison of Des Moines, Iowa, is credited with developing the first electric vehicle in the United States in 1890–91. In the United States, electric cars started to be produced commercially in 1896 by **American Electric Vehicle** of Chicago and **Pope Manufacturing Company** of Boston. Between 1896 and 1928, at least fifty-four different companies were manufacturing electric cars.

Electric cars were popular as urban delivery vehicles and for doctors. This was because the vehicle could go for fifty to one hundred miles without a recharge and could easily stop and start many times, as one does when making deliveries. In 1900, three hundred electric taxicabs were operating in New York City.

In Detroit, **Century Electric** made electric cars from 1912 to 1915. It manufactured open body roadsters, which sold for $1,250 in 1912, and enclosed broughams, like opera coaches. The company's cars had an "underslung frame" that distinguished it from other electrics and helped them sell for a few years, but the unique frames were not enough to save the company from bankruptcy in 1915.

The **Flanders Electric Company** produced an electric car in Pontiac that was engineered by and named for Walter Flanders, the "F" in the **E-M-F Company**. He had formerly been Henry Ford's production manager. **Flanders Electric Company** made both electric- and gasoline-powered cars in its factory. The Flanders 6 was the company's most notable electric model and sold for $1,775 to $2,500. The engine was underneath the car, so there was no need for a hood; therefore, the Flanders Electric did not have one. The car never caught on even though Walter Flanders spent more than $1 million in advertising. The company went into receivership in 1914 after producing less than one hundred cars. Walter Flanders moved on to become one of the founders of the **Maxwell Motor Company**.

The **Grinnell Electric Car Company** manufactured electric cars from 1912 until 1915. Looking to the high end of the market, their autos sold from $2,800 to $3,400 and were primarily broughams and closed body coupes. The owners, the Grinnell brothers, dissolved the company to become the Grinnell Brothers Piano Company because selling pianos and other musical instruments was proving more profitable for them than the electric cars. They produced a small obituary for their electric car company for automotive trade publications in January 1916 and then went on selling musical instruments for many years after.

Detroit Electric Outsells and Outlives All the Rest

The **Detroit Electric Car Company** started out in Port Huron as the **Anderson Carriage Company**. Founder William C. Anderson started making horse-drawn carriages and buggies in 1884 in Port Huron. In 1895, Anderson moved the carriage company factory to the corner of Riopelle and Clay Streets in Detroit. It produced 160,000 carriages before Anderson decided that the future was in automobiles. He ceased carriage and buggy production, fired all his employees, scrapped the machinery and began making electric cars. One of the most long-lived electric car companies, it operated from 1907 to 1939, producing a car called the Detroit Electric.

The battery of the Detroit Electric was a rechargeable lead-acid battery. An Edison nickel-iron battery was available for an extra $600, and the

One of the Detroit Electric recharge stations for electric cars was on 110 Grand Boulevard near Jefferson in the early 1900s. *Courtesy of LeAnne Rubino.*

Detroit Electric could go as far as 211 miles on a single charge of the Edison battery. The main disadvantage of the Detroit Electric car was that it could only go about 20 miles per hour, although this was considered adequate for city driving in the early Brass Era of autos.

Through the 1910s, Detroit Electric was at its peak, selling one to two thousand vehicles per year. The high gasoline prices during World War I were a boon to electric cars such as Detroit Electric, since it didn't need gas for fuel. **Detroit Electric Car Company** kept producing cars on a fairly large scale until the stock market crash of 1929. It declared bankruptcy, and founder William Anderson died that year, although Detroit Electric cars were custom-built for customers through the 1930s, producing about ten cars a year from the city's smallest auto factory at 731 Tenth Street in Detroit. The last one was produced in 1939, although they were available until 1942.

The electric cars' popularity was fading by the 1920s as gasoline-powered cars took the lead among the buying public. The invention of the electric ignition, doing away with hand-cranking, did much to enhance the sales of gasoline-powered vehicles. Gasoline vehicles were faster and didn't have the limited driving range electric cars had. Electric car batteries were expensive to maintain and replace. They were also very heavy, which tended to wear down the tires more than other vehicles.

Over the years, quiet engines and clean power have brought electric cars back into prominence at various times, but they have never again achieved the market percentage they had in the early 1900s.

THE RISE OF DETROIT'S
MILWAUKEE JUNCTION

Although many of the Indiana and Ohio companies lasted for years, by the time the gasoline auto had begun to assert its dominance in 1910, the road to the parts manufacturers and auto companies continually led to Detroit. By 1915, all the top cars in the United States were produced in Detroit.

Many of the auto companies of the early 1900s got their start in the area of Detroit known as Milwaukee Junction. This area was at the crossroads of two railroad companies. As more auto companies came into the area, many parts manufacturers, such as **Fisher Body**, built factories in the district. The boundaries of the Milwaukee Junction area in Detroit are usually given as East Grand Boulevard to the north, St. Aubin Street and Hamtramck Drive to the east, Woodward Avenue to the west and the border following I-94 to I-75 to Warren Road to the south. Milwaukee Street ran through the center of the area.

Henry Ford's first successful company, the third one he started, opened in Milwaukee Junction as the **Ford Motor Company**. It was in this factory on Piquette Avenue that he developed the most popular Ford car, the Model T. He also fine-tuned his assembly line process there.

Other auto companies starting in this area included the **Paige-Detroit Motor Car Company**; **Everitt, Metzger & Flanders (E-M-F)**; **Hupp**; **Brush Motor Car Company**; **Anderson Electric Car Company**; **Cadillac**; **Dodge Brothers**; **Oakland**; **Studebaker**; and **Packard**.

PAIGE

THE MOST BEAUTIFUL CAR IN AMERICA

A MAN'S MOTOR CAR is one of his personal possessions. If it is commonplace it stamps him as a man of little or no discrimination. If it is "gaudy," it proclaims his bad taste and lack of refinement.

As a consequence, well-bred people insist upon a compromise between these two extremes.

They demand individuality in their Motor Cars. But it is the quiet, unpretentious individuality that characterizes a Patrician the world over. They demand "smartness" in their Motor Cars—but it is the smartness of exquisite design, luxurious appointment and finished detail.

In a word, they demand just such a car as the Paige—"The Most Beautiful Car in America."

PAIGE-DETROIT MOTOR CAR CO., DETROIT
Manufacturers of Motor Cars and Motor Trucks

Above: The **Ford Motor Company** Piquette Street plant was located in the Milwaukee Junction area and was where Ford developed the Model T. *Courtesy of the Ford Piquette Museum.*

Left: **Paige** was an auto manufacturing company with its factory near the Milwaukee Junction area. It billed itself as "the most beautiful car in America." *Author's collection.*

34

THE HUPP MOTOR COMPANY SENDS THREE MEN TO DRIVE AROUND THE WORLD

Robert C. Hupp (1878–1931) was born in Grand Rapids, Michigan, in 1878. He moved to Detroit and attended high school there while he worked for the **Olds Motor Works**. He continued to work for Olds as R.E. Olds moved the factory to Lansing. Taking a nine-month detour from auto manufacturing to travel to Chicago to work for a soda fountain manufacturer, Hupp came back to Detroit and got a job working for the **Ford Motor Company**, where he teamed up with John Dodge on **Ford**'s Model K. He quit there in 1907 to work for the **Regal Motor Company** before constructing a four-cylinder, lightweight auto and forming the **Hupp Motor Car Company** in 1908. Production on his namesake car began in 1909. By 1910, he had sold more than five thousand units. The **Hupp** factory was at 345 Bellevue Avenue in Detroit.

Robert Hupp's most well-known publicity stunt involved having three men drive a Hupmobile around the world. The trip was immortalized in a book titled *Three Men in a Hupp: Around the World by Automobile, 1910–1912*. The venture would have helped sell a lot more Hupmobiles overseas if the **Hupp Motor Car Company** had not stopped making the model that executed the round-the-world voyage so well. That model performed well because it was light and could be easily extricated from the various pitfalls it fell into in foreign lands, including streets not designed for motorcars and bad roads in general (or, in many cases, no roads).

By the time the three men in the Hupp had completed their voyage in 1912, Hupp was already working on his next venture. Disagreements about building a more luxurious car and discontinuing the smaller model caused Robert Hupp to sell his stock and quit his namesake company in 1911. He was not in favor of building the larger cars. He went on to form the **Hupp-Yeats Electric Car Company** with his brother, Louis. The company produced electric cars at 110 Lycaste Street in Detroit from 1911 to 1916. The company's electric cars had five selective speeds and could seat four people in either an open or closed model. The car's battery could take the vehicle seventy-five to ninety miles before requiring a recharge, a good deal for the day. The **Hupp-Yeats Electric Car Company** produced a vehicle that looked like a luxury carriage. They called it an "electric coach" with the model names Imperial and Royal, leaving no doubt what market they were appealing to.

The old **Hupp Motor Car Company** took the new one to court, saying the new company's name caused confusion. The court agreed that the **Hupp-Yeats Electric Car Company**'s name was too similar to the older company. Even Robert claiming the new company wasn't named for himself but for his brother, Louis, didn't fly with the court. Robert Hupp was forced to use his initials and change the name of the company to the **RCH Company**. This was much like Ransom E. Olds when he had to use his initials instead of his last name to form the **REO Motor Company**. The **RCH Company** started off well in 1912 with its electric car but tried to produce too many by the next year and had quality problems. The year 1914 was the last one of production, as the electric car was losing in popularity.

In 1913, Robert C. Hupp again left a company he had founded and joined the **Monarch Motor Car Company**. The **Hupp-Yeats Electric Car Company** continued on until 1919, when it was purchased by a group of investors. In 1920, the company was discontinued.

The original **Hupp Motor Car Company** continued to grow and produce autos until 1924, when it purchased a larger factory to continue its increasing production. Sales topped sixty-five thousand units in 1928, and in 1929, it purchased the **Chandler Motor Company**, mainly to use its factories to produce more Hupmobiles.

The **Hupp Motor Car Company** changed its marketing strategy in 1925 by aiming chiefly for the luxury market with its new eight-cylinder models. Retooling for the six different brands became a costly undertaking and cut into **Hupp**'s profit margin.

The 1932 Hupp Comet was a popular sports model that came in fifth in the Indy 500 that year. In 1936, the company sold some of its plants but in 1938 introduced a new model, the Skylark. The Skylark helped, but by 1939, production was less than one thousand units.

A short association with the **Graham-Paige** saw the last Hupp Skylarks produced by **Graham-Paige** in 1940. In 1941, the **Hupp** company came out of bankruptcy after shedding its auto plants. It continued as **Hupp, Inc.,** manufacturing air-conditioning and industrial heating units.

Although Robert Hupp ended up leaving both his namesake companies, he did try once more with another company, **Monarch Motor Car Company**. His later car companies were not as successful or as long-lived as his original company, but Robert Hupp also owned a number of successful businesses. His other companies put together car parts and included a foundry, a machine company and a forge company. After leaving **Monarch**, Hupp assisted **Chrysler Corporation** with new innovations.

The Hupmobile was known as a rugged automobile capable of making round-the-world trips but by 1934, to the chagrin of many, was designed to be a luxury car, as pictured. *Photo by the author.*

The **Monarch Motor Car Company** was started by Robert and Louis Hupp's brother-in-law Joseph Bloom in 1913. Robert Hupp designed a small four-cylinder car and also another one with a V-8 engine for the company. Investors didn't come through, and by 1914, the company was bankrupt. Robert Hupp's brother, Louis, had a similar experience with the **Tribune Motor Company** in 1913, producing a car called the Tribune. It was a small four-cylinder car that had a limited production due to financing not coming through.

C.H. BLOMSTROM

If at First You Don't Succeed, Quit and Start a New Company

Carl H. Blomstrom (1867–1923) was born in Grand Rapids and received a degree in engineering in 1884. Working at an engine company in Marquette, Michigan, he built his first car in 1897. It had a two-cylinder, air-cooled engine. Blomstrom built his next car in 1899 and moved to Detroit in 1901 to design and build gasoline-powered engines in a factory at 64 Second Street.

By 1902, Blomstrom started manufacturing a one-cylinder car called the Blomstrom. By the end of the year, he had built two dozen cars in a factory at Leib and Wright Streets in Detroit. He shared the factory with the **Griswold Motor Company**. J.P. La Vigne, who had worked for the **Detroit Automobile Company**, designed the Griswold. In 1907, the **Griswold Motor Company** was incorporated and its first cars were on the road. The Griswold was a ten-horsepower, three-passenger runabout. After sharing a factory, the company was purchased by the **C.H. Blomstrom Motor Car Company** when it declared bankruptcy at the end of 1907.

Blomstrom released a more advanced two-cylinder car than the previous one-cylinder car in 1903. In 1904, Blomstrom formed the **C.H. Blomstrom Motor Car Company** and moved it to a nineteen-acre factory complex at 75 Clark Avenue on River Road in Detroit. They manufactured a car there named the Queen, which was a two-passenger runabout, available with either a one- or two-cylinder engine. In 1906, troubles with the incorporation led to the **C.H. Blomstrom Motor Car Company** combining with the **De Luxe Motor Company**.

The joint venture of the two companies lasted until 1909, when both went out of business. Blomstrom had developed a car called the Gyroscope, the design of which was purchased by the **Lion Motor Car Company** of Adrian, Michigan. **Lion** produced the Gyroscope in 1909. It discontinued that model in 1910 to produce the **Lion** until 1912. The **Lion Motor Car Company** was a successful company until a fire burned down its plant at the end of 1912—destroying two hundred cars and causing the company o go out of business.

Blomstrom was back in late 1913 with the **Rex Motor Company** in Detroit. The Rex was a four-cylinder, fourteen-horsepower vehicle capable of traveling forty-five miles per hour with a water-cooled "cyclecar" designed by Blomstrom and priced at $395. The venture didn't make it much further than the drawing board, and by 1914, Blomstrom was on his way to New Jersey and the **Bateman Manufacturing Company** to design a car called the Frontmobile.

In 1901, the **Kirk Manufacturing Company** consolidated and in 1903 brought out a car called the Yale that was built in Toledo, Ohio. It was a five-passenger touring car with a water-cooled sixteen-horsepower, two-cylinder engine and wasn't changed throughout the three years it was produced. Its slogan was "The Beau Brummell of the Road." The company failed, and in 1906, the factory was taken over by the **De Luxe Motor Company** of

Detroit. **De Luxe** used the factory to produce its De Luxe auto, a luxury model with roller bearings on the crankshaft and a four-cylinder engine with sixty horsepower selling for $4,750. The company also continued producing the Queen auto of its partners, the **C.H. Blomstrom Motor Car Company**. **De Luxe** then moved its entire operation to Detroit from Toledo. When the **De Luxe Motor Company** failed in 1909, the company's Detroit plant was acquired by the **E-M-F Company**.

The **Wayne Automobile Company** started in Detroit in 1904. It was formed by Charles Palms, grandson of Francis Palms, at one time the largest landowner in Michigan. The car was officially named for General "Mad" Anthony Wayne, a hero of the Revolutionary War and other skirmishes. The **Wayne Automobile Company** had five different models of automobiles, ranging from two-seaters with two-cylinder engines to fifty-horsepower vehicles with four-cylinder engines.

The car was designed by William Kelly and was his second try at car building. The first car he designed was called the Kelly, and when placed on the road in 1901, it was judged to vibrate too much. The second car, the Wayne, solved the problems of the first and was a two-cylinder, water-cooled, gasoline-fueled model that hit the road in 1904. The 1905 Wayne was a touring model with a detachable rear tonneau. The 1907 Wayne was a seven-passenger vehicle with a four-cylinder engine. Called the R Model, it came with five lamps and a generator. The Wayne factory was at Brush and Piquette Streets in the Milwaukee Junction and was a three-story, forty- by six-hundred-foot brick building situated on five acres.

Three Superstar Auto Men Form E-M-F Company

In 1907, Byron Everitt became the president of **Wayne Automobile Company** and sold his **Everitt Carriage Trimming Company** to Walter O. Briggs. Briggs started the **Briggs Manufacturing Company** in 1908 to supply auto bodies to auto companies. He also acquired the Detroit Tigers baseball team from previous owner Frank Navin's family when Navin died in 1935. Tiger Stadium was known as Navin Field until 1938, when it was changed to Briggs Stadium. It was renamed Tiger Stadium in 1961.

In early 1908, Walter Flanders left **Ford Motor Company** and became the manager at **Wayne Automobile Company**. When Flanders joined with Byron Everitt and William Metzger of the **Northern Manufacturing**

The headquarters and plant of the **E-M-F Company** in Detroit, the number two car company in 1911. *Author's collection.*

Company, the three became partners and combined the **Wayne** and **Northern** companies to form the **E-M-F Company**.

The **E-M-F Company** was named with the initials of the founders, Byron "Barney" Everitt, William Metzger and Walter Flanders. All three brought different auto building skills to the table. Barney Everitt got his start building carriages, William Metzger was a salesperson and Walter Flanders was a machinist. In 1909, they came together to build their own distinctive automobiles.

Unfortunately, the 1909 models had many mechanical flaws that detractors were quick to capitalize on, saying that the E-M-F in **E-M-F Company** stood for "Every Morning Fix-It," "Every Mechanic's Friend," "Every Morning Frustration" and other damning phrases. **E-M-F** had entered into an agreement with the **Studebaker Corporation** to sell its cars through the Studebaker network. When the mechanical faults of the **E-M-F** cars that **Studebaker** sold came to light, the president of **Studebaker**, Fred Fish, decreed that **Studebaker** would send its mechanics out and fix the flaws free of charge.

The cars sold through **Studebaker** were branded as "E-M-F Studebaker." The **Studebaker** agreement caused internal bickering among the three principals of **E-M-F** as to the future role **Studebaker** would take in the company. The rifts were never settled to the satisfaction of all, and the company was short-lived. By 1911, the **E-M-F Company** was controlled by Fred Fish, president of **Studebaker** and son-in-law of the founder.

Despite its problems, the 1909 **E-M-F** was the fourth top-selling car company in the United States for the year, right behind **Ford**, **Buick** and **Maxwell**. A then independent **Cadillac Automobile Company** was fifth. In 1910, **E-M-F** held on to its fourth-place finish, this time behind **Ford**, **Buick** and **Overland**. In 1911, the company was number two behind **Ford**. In 1912 and thereafter, the cars were badged as Studebaker/ E-M-F and then just Studebaker. The principals of **E-M-F** would later meet again with the formation of the **Rickenbacker Motor Company**.

WHEELBARROW JOHNNY AND THE RISE OF STUDEBAKER

An early resident of Milwaukee Junction was the **Studebaker Corporation**. It was another company that started as a wagon and buggy manufacturer. The chief organizer was John Studebaker, who was the third eldest son in the family. John caught gold fever in 1849 and went to Placerville, California. He was too late to get in on any of the good mining locations, so instead of gold prospecting, he started making wheelbarrows and had a successful business of selling them to the prospectors. He was known as "Wheelbarrow Johnny."

In 1852, "Wheelbarrow Johnny" Studebaker moved to South Bend, Indiana, where his brothers Henry and Clem were blacksmiths and proprietors of the successful **Studebaker Wagon Corporation**. (Abe Lincoln rode in a Studebaker carriage the night of his assassination.) John had $8,000 of funds and joined with his brothers in 1868 to form the **Studebaker Brothers Manufacturing Company** with himself as president.

By 1901, John Studebaker, at age sixty-eight, was the sole remaining Studebaker brother. He traveled to Chicago, where he saw electric cars. His son-in-law Fred Fish, who was a former New Jersey state senator and had married John Studebaker's daughter Grace, thought that electric cars would be the next big thing and convinced John to build and sell twenty battery-powered vehicles in 1902. Fish would also get Studebaker involved in gasoline-powered autos. Fish became president of Studebaker in 1909 and, later, chairman of the board from 1915 to 1935.

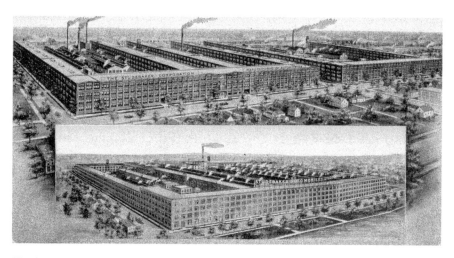

The **Studebaker Corporation** moved from Detroit to South Bend, Indiana, where it also had an eight-hundred-acre proving ground for road-testing the new autos. *Author's collection.*

The **Studebaker** plants in the Milwaukee Junction at Clark Street and at West Jefferson Avenue in Detroit produced over fifty thousand vehicles. *Author's collection.*

In 1904, Arthur Garford of Elysia, Ohio, an inventor who made a fortune with his padded bicycle seat, entered into an agreement with Studebaker and the Studebaker-Garford was born—an auto with a Studebaker body and a Garford engine and chassis marketed as a "horseless carriage." In

1908, Studebaker purchased a third of the **E-M-F Company** and by 1909 had made $9.5 million in profits. In 1910, it purchased the rest of **E-M-F** from the J.P. Morgan Company and effectively took over the company. John Studebaker died at the age of eighty-three.

After the war, Fred Fish continued as president of the company and guided it through both prosperous and lean years, including the merger with **Packard** in 1955.

Henry Ford's Second Company Becomes Cadillac Automobile Company

The **Cadillac Automobile Company** was a separate company before it became a division of **GM**. It got its start through another Big Three principal, Henry Ford, who had won a big race, the Grosse Pointe Sweepstakes Race, in 1901. He used this victory to raise funds and start his second auto company, the **Henry Ford Company**. His first company, the Detroit Automobile Company, had run aground after producing a mail delivery wagon but little more. However, after Ford's race car scored a lot of wins, many of the original investors signed back on.

Ford hired Oliver Barthel as his main assistant. Barthel had previous experience with **Mohawk Motor Company**, later called **Lafayette Motor Company**. Barthel designed a two-cylinder engine, but Henry Ford quit the company in March 1902 because Barthel and others wanted to enter production sooner than Ford was ready. After Ford left the company, it was liquidated in October 1902.

Henry Leland (1843–1932) was born in Vermont and studied in Rhode Island before joining Colt Manufacturing Company in Connecticut to work on firearms. After starting a machine shop called **Leland and Faulconer**, he started developing his own gasoline engine designs. Moving to the Detroit area, he began selling engines to the **Olds Motor Works**. He also invented the first electric barber clippers.

In 1902, Leland came to survey the plant at 1363 Cass Avenue in Detroit and came away with an agreement to form a new company with the old **Henry Ford Company** investors. The new company would use the more efficient engine Leland had developed and would be named the **Cadillac Automobile Company** after the founder of Detroit, Antoine Cadillac. This seemed like a good idea since Detroit had just celebrated its 200th

Pictured are two models of Cadillac: the 1906 Tulip Body Touring Car and the 1909 model. Cadillac was already a top seller before it became part of **General Motors**. *Author's collection.*

anniversary in 1901 and the name Cadillac was once again fresh in the public's mind. So the **Cadillac Automobile Company** came about as a remnant of Henry Ford's second failed auto company.

By 1903, Cadillac's success put **Cadillac Automobile Company** in the number two position of automakers that year, with only the **Olds Motor Works** ahead of it. Henry Leland remained in charge, and by 1905 the Cadillac had a four-cylinder engine. The Cadillac was a well-admired vehicle, and consumer demand for it was more than **Cadillac** could build. The company, with Leland at the helm, pioneered using interchangeable parts.

In 1909, Billy Durant acquired the **Cadillac Automobile Company** for **GM**. Cadillac went on to become the longest surviving nameplate for **GM**. It has not changed its image as a luxury car since production began more than one hundred years ago.

Leland was in charge of the Cadillac division of **GM** until 1917. While there, he helped develop an electric starter for the Cadillac. At the onset of World War I, Leland left **GM** after a dispute with Billy Durant. He got a grant and formed the **Lincoln Motor Company** to develop the V-12 aircraft engine. After the war, the company began producing luxury autos.

Producing finely styled autos until facing bankruptcy in 1922, the **Lincoln Motor Company** was purchased by **Ford Motor Company** for $8 million and became the luxury car division within the company.

So Leland was the creator of the luxury car marque for both **GM** and **Ford**. Leland continued to operate the Lincoln division until Henry Ford fired him a few years later. Leland lived to be eighty-nine.

GRAHAM-PAIGE BUILT A BIGGER AUTO

In the early days of automobile manufacturing, autos were considered a "rich man's toy" because so many of the first companies manufactured luxury automobiles. The **Paige-Detroit Motor Car Company** was no exception, as it produced luxury automobiles from 1908 until 1927, starting in a Milwaukee Junction–area factory. It was founded by Frederick Osgood Paige, who had been the president of **Reliance Motor Company** prior to its takeover by **GM**. The **Reliance Motor Company** started independently building trucks in Detroit in 1902 and became the truck division of **GM** known as **GMC**.

The company needed money to move forward and called on Henry M. Jewett, who made a fortune in coal mining, to be the company's financier. He joined **Paige-Detroit Motor Car Company** in 1909 and pronounced the first year's output as "rotten and pieces of junk." In 1910, Jewett shut down production and cleaned house, replacing Fred Paige as president with himself and hiring all new engineers. Keeping the name Paige, the result was the 1911 Paige Roadster. This car was powered by a twenty-five-horsepower, four-cylinder engine. In 1912, the company produced different models using the names of Brooklands, Beverly, Kenilworth, Rockland, LaMarquise and Brunswick. The first six-cylinder Paige came out in 1915, and by 1916 all models had six-cylinder engines. The Paige was advertised as the "Most Beautiful Car in America," and in 1921 a Paige won the Daytona 500.

The 1922 Paige Daytona was a popular model, and in the same year, a smaller version was produced and called the Jewett, after Henry Jewett. The **Paige-Detroit Motor Car Company** was a successful enterprise through 1925, when production pushed past forty thousand vehicles per year. By 1926, production had slowed, and Henry Jewett was tiring of the auto industry. The company was sold to the Graham brothers—Joseph, Ray and Robert. The Graham brothers had just ended their association with the **Dodge Brothers Motor Company** and its truck division.

The Graham brothers started with a glass factory their father, Ziba Foote Graham, and his eldest son, Joseph, had purchased in 1905 and called the

Southern Indiana Glass Company. In 1907, they renamed it the Graham Bottle Company when Robert joined the firm. The last Graham brother, Ray, joined in 1908. Joseph had made improvements on the bottle-making process by the time they purchased a giant bottle plant in Evansville, Indiana. By 1915, the Grahams were the largest beer and soda pop bottle manufacturers in the United States and opened two new glass-producing plants in Oklahoma.

Two other successful glass manufacturers, Michael Owens and Edward Libbey, had merged their operations to form Libbey-Owens Sheet Glass Company. They purchased Graham Bottle Company and Joseph's bottle-making patents, keeping the Graham name as a subsidiary. This left the Graham brothers free to form a new company, **Graham Brothers, Inc.** They started building farm tractors in a factory in Evansville, Indiana, as well as a kit that converted a Model T Ford into a light truck. By late 1919, they branched out into producing their own truck. This was a one-and-a-half-ton-capacity vehicle called the Graham Speed Truck.

The Grahams started using **Dodge** engines because of their high quality and entered into an agreement in 1921 with the **Dodge Brothers Motor Company** to provide engines and transmissions to the Grahams while giving the **Dodge** sales dealerships exclusive rights to sell the Graham trucks. **Graham Brothers, Inc.** opened an assembly plant on Meldrum Avenue in Detroit in early 1922. When sales warranted additional production, the company acquired the old **King Motor Car Company** factory on Conant Avenue in Detroit in late 1922. In 1923, the Grahams still needed additional space, so they started using the old **Dodge** plant on Lynch Road in Detroit. When this still proved inadequate, they added plants in Stockton, California, and Toronto, Ontario, in Canada. By 1926, the Grahams were the largest independent truck producers in the world. In 1924, the **Dodge Brothers** purchased the **Graham Brothers, Inc.** truck operation.

In 1927, the Graham brothers purchased the **Paige-Detroit Motor Car Company**, which was still producing autos named the Paige and the Jewett. They paid $4 million. The Graham brothers were not legally allowed to manufacture trucks anymore due to their separation agreement with the **Dodge Brothers Motor Company**, so they were happy to find a car company to purchase since manufacturing autos wouldn't break their agreement.

The Graham brothers restructured the **Paige-Detroit Motor Car Company** and renamed it the **Graham-Paige Motors Corporation**. In 1928, the new company brought out its new vehicle, the Graham-Paige, at the New York Automobile Show, in a lavish affair at the Roosevelt Hotel. Boxer Gene Tunney and Notre Dame football coach Knute Rockne were the featured speakers. The year 1928 was also a banner year for production—the company produced 73,195 autos, a new record. The new motto was "See how 50 miles an hour feels like 38. Drive a new Graham-Paige today."

After the 1930 line of cars, "Paige" was dropped from the car name, although the corporation retained the company name. The cars were known as "Grahams" thereafter. The Graham brothers saw sales fall drastically as the Great Depression hit in the 1930s, but the **Graham-Paige Motors Corporation** stayed in business until 1940, when the factory was retooled for World War II military production.

Products were in scarce supply after the war, resulting from years of sending the best of the needed products across the ocean to Europe and the Pacific Islands in the form of airplanes and tanks. Rather than returning those armed vehicles to the United States for recycling, the equipment was mostly destroyed and left behind. After the war, the **Graham-Paige Corporation** decided it no longer wanted to produce automobiles. The

The first **Graham-Paige** plant at 8505 West Warren in Dearborn is pictured in its later incarnation as a car dealership. The 8505 West Warren location in Detroit was the factory where **Graham-Paige** conducted a joint venture with Hupmobile. *Author's collection.*

decision was based on the high costs of retooling war production factories, acquiring raw materials and laying out capital to process pre-production designs to begin manufacturing new autos. Therefore, Joe Frazer, along with industrialist Henry J. Kaiser, acquired the company.

Joseph Washington Frazer (1892–1971) was an auto mechanic, salesman and a top executive in a number of different auto companies. He was responsible for the naming of what became a top division of **Chrysler Corporation**—Plymouth Motors. The company wanted to produce a lower-end vehicle that would appeal to farmers.

While talking to top executive Walter Chrysler about what to name the new vehicle, Frazer asked, "How about Plymouth?" This was met with guffaws of laughter by the other executives.

"Why would anyone name a car Plymouth?" one of the execs asked.

"Because it's a trusted name among farmers—most of them already buy a product called Plymouth Binder Twine," replied the savvy Frazer.

Walter Chrysler, once a farmer himself, agreed and said, "Every farmer in America knows about Plymouth Binder Twine. Let's give them a name they're familiar with."

Plymouth became one of **Chrysler**'s most successful brands. Although inspired by the twine product name, an early badge featured Plymouth Rock, 1620 arrival point for pilgrims in Massachusetts.

Frazer spent many successful years at **Chrysler**, and in 1939, he was elected president of the **Willys-Overland Motor Company**. The Willys Overland was the second top-selling car company from 1912 to 1918 (behind **Ford Motor Company**).

With Frazer in the top position, the company received the contract from the U.S. government to produce the General Purpose (GP) military utility vehicle. The name Jeep came from the "GP" portion. During World War II, the Jeep was known to be flexible and durable. When offered to the public after the war, it was a success as a civilian work vehicle and brought the **Willys Company** back to prominence.

When Joe Frazer left **Willys** in 1944, the company's yearly sales topped $21 million. Frazer then assumed control of the **Graham-Paige Motors Corporation** when he partnered with Henry J. Kaiser and bought the controlling interest in the stock. Henry Kaiser (1892–1967) was known for shipbuilding, Kaiser Aluminum, Kaiser Steel and Kaiser Hospitals. Frazer and Kaiser renamed the company the **Kaiser-Frazer Motor Company**. Joseph Frazer was named president of the company in 1945.

A more modern view of the original **Graham-Paige** plant, now in use as a bakery company. The factory was also used to produce the Paige car, the Jewett, named for the company's president. *Photo by the author.*

The **Willys-Overland Company** headquarters was in this building in Toledo, Ohio, when Joe Frazer became president. It was one of the largest industrial office buildings in the world in its day. *Author's collection.*

The military car called the Jeep was also a flexible work vehicle for civilians after World War II. *Author's collection.*

The **Kaiser-Frazer** assembly line produced the Kaiser and the Frazer models. *Author's collection.*

The **Graham-Paige** company had its main factory on West Warren Avenue by the Detroit Terminal Railroad. The plant encompassed 721,430 square feet. *Author's collection.*

The 1946 auto offering was called the Frazer, after Joe Frazer. There was also a less expensive version named the Kaiser, for Henry Kaiser. The company acquired a former aircraft plant called Willow Run between Belleville and Ypsilanti (not far from Detroit) where the vehicles were assembled.

Joseph Frazer left the **Kaiser-Frazer Motor Company** in 1948 after one too many disputes with Henry Kaiser, and the company was reorganized as the **Kaiser Motor Company**. In 1953, **Kaiser Motor Company** announced the purchase of the Jeep and the **Willys Company**. The last Kaiser passenger car rolled off the line in 1956 (the Frazer car was phased out in 1951). However, the **Kaiser-Jeep Corporation** division continued to produce Jeeps and kept the company profitable for more than a decade.

Finally, the **Kaiser Motor Company** wished to divest its auto division and sold the Jeep division to the **American Motors Company** in 1970. In 1989 the brand name became the property of **Chrysler Corporation** (and subsequently **Daimler** and **Fiat**) when **Chrysler** purchased the assets of **AMC**.

Charles Brady King

Inventor of the First Car in Detroit

Charles Brady King (1868–1957), the first man to drive a car down the streets of Detroit, started the **Northern Manufacturing Company** with Jonathan Maxwell, later to start **Maxwell Motor Company**, in 1902. Both men had previously worked for the **Olds Motor Works**. The **Northern Manufacturing Company** became the forerunner of the **Maxwell** and **Chrysler** auto companies. The first model was a two-seater roundabout in 1904, called the Northern, and it had a one-cylinder, five-horsepower engine.

Maxwell jumped ship two years later and formed the **Maxwell-Briscoe Motor Company** with former **Buick** executive Benjamin Briscoe. King went on to pioneer left-hand steering and air-operated pneumatic brakes on the 1906 model, which had a four-cylinder engine. For the 1908 model, King incorporated all the operating controls on the steering column of a limousine version, the first instance of the modern dashboard.

The Duryea brothers were among the first auto manufacturers. The 1909 Stevens-Duryea Touring Car was built to carry seven passengers comfortably. The aluminum body, six-cylinder car sold for over $4,000. *Author's collection.*

In 1907, a plant opened in Port Huron, Michigan, to produce the two-cylinder version of the Northern while the Detroit factory produced the four-cylinder version. The 1908 Northerns—models B, C and L—were the last produced under the Northern name. The **Northern Manufacturing Company** merged with the **Wayne Automobile Company** in 1908. Soon thereafter, both companies were absorbed into **E-M-F**, and the Northern nameplate was history.

Charles Brady King went on to form the **King Motor Car Company** in 1911. After he resigned from the **Northern Manufacturing Company**, he went to Europe for two years to study auto styling. When he returned, he rented a factory at 1559 West Jefferson Street in Detroit and started producing the King 35. That model was proclaimed the most modern car of the day because of its four-cylinder engine and three-speed gear system. With a cover over the exhaust pipe, the car was rendered more silent than most—popular features, since most cars of the day were excessively noisy. Those additions, along with pedal-operated brakes, helped the King become a popular model.

In 1911, as the **King Motor Car Company** moved into the old Hupmobile factory at 1300–24 Jefferson Avenue and Concord Street, it ran

Above: The 1917 King Roadster had an eight-cylinder engine and was produced while Charles King was serving with the Signal Corp during World War I. *Author's collection.*

Left: The **Krit Motor Car Company** used a symbol that would later be reviled as one of the symbols of the Nazis—the swastika. *Courtesy of James Ball.*

into some financial trouble. Chewing gum magnate Artemus Ward from New York City bought the company outright and manufactured autos under the King marque in Detroit until 1923. During this time, the King became the first auto to include a horn and a clock as standard equipment. In 1923, a group of investors purchased the company and moved operations to Buffalo, New York, where the company produced a small number of Kings—only 240 for 1923 and 1924—before entering into bankruptcy. In 1925, the cars that were still left in stock were sold in England.

King's fate was preceded by the demise of **Krit Motor Car Company**, which was in trouble, historically speaking, from the start, when it decided to use the swastika as its car symbol, even though it was a good twenty years before the Nazi Party of Germany adopted the symbol.

The **Krit Motor Car Company** was established in 1909 by Claude S. Briggs and was named for the first few letters of chief engineer Kenneth Crittenden. The former factory of the **C.H. Blomstrom Motor Car Company** at Leib and Wright Streets was secured for use to build its four-cylinder auto with a sliding gear transmission. The company struggled but was able to raise more capital to lease a larger facility at 1620 East Grand Boulevard. In 1913, a six-cylinder car was introduced and, in 1915, so was a more streamlined body. However, the **Krit Motor Car Company** had financial problems and, in 1915, was forced into bankruptcy by its creditors.

EDDIE RICKENBACKER

Aviator and Auto Maker

Eddie Rickenbacker (1890–1973) first came into prominence during World War I when he had twenty-six aerial victories and was awarded the Congressional Medal of Honor. The author of four books, he was an executive at Eastern Air Lines during that company's formative years. He became part of auto history as the one-time owner of the Indianapolis Speedway and his Detroit auto venture, the **Rickenbacker Motor Company**. After he quit the auto company, he once again served his country in World War II and was famously in a plane that crash-landed in the Pacific Ocean. Rickenbacker and the crew survived for twenty-four days on life rafts before they were rescued. He died in 1973 at the age of eighty-three.

The **Rickenbacker Motor Company** started in 1921 when Eddie Rickenbacker met one of the founders of the **E-M-F Company**, Barney Everitt. Rickenbacker had been entertaining publishing and motion picture offers after World War I had made him a national hero. When Everitt suggested Rickenbacker head a car company, Everitt struck the right chord with the aviator. Everitt called his old friend Walt Flanders from **E-M-F**. Flanders at first refused because he wanted to retire after saving **Maxwell Motor Company** from the **United States Motor Company's** bankruptcy. However, he let Everitt talk him into it and became a vice-president of the new company with Everitt as president. Rickenbacker himself declined the presidency to be a vice-president and head of public relations. The other **E-M-F** principal, Billy Metzger, could not be talked out of his retirement other than in an occasional advisory capacity. The rest of the principals were all people with years of experience in the auto field.

Rickenbacker wanted his car to be "worthy of the name" and took a long time road testing and improving the prototype. Finally, in 1921, he was happy, and the company was incorporated. A new plant was designed by architect Albert Kahn at 4815 Cabot Avenue in Detroit.

The Rickenbacker autos came in sedan, touring and coupe models with a price of $1,500 and a top speed of sixty-five miles per hour. At first, there were a few problems; for instance, the gas gauge was wired to the battery, which slowly drained battery power. If the car went a couple of days without being driven, the battery would die. This problem was resolved by attaching the gas gauge to a lamp that had to be turned on to read the gauge.

The car maker's 1923 models were essentially a carryover from the 1922 models. Rickenbacker, in his role as public relations manager, visited all the forty-four distributorships and 250 dealers that the auto company had. He also met with more than one thousand Rickenbacker auto owners.

Tragedy struck in 1925 when Walter Flanders was killed in an auto accident. More turmoil ensued when the **Rickenbacker Motor Company** announced that the next year's vehicles would have four-wheel brakes. Some of the companies that only had two-wheel brakes started a controversy by claiming that four-wheel brakes were unsafe. They even went so far as to issue bumper stickers that said "Beware four-wheel brakes."

The adverse publicity and the loss of Flander's guidance took its toll on the company, and by the end of 1924, it was posting big losses. In February

The **Rickenbacker Motor Company** factory, designed by Albert Kahn, as it looks in 2015. *Photo by the author.*

1925, the company announced a new six-cylinder engine for passenger cars and an eight-cylinder for race cars. In 1926, reduced prices meant reduced profits for dealers, and they complained. Soon, stockholders and directors began to battle and at times blamed Eddie Rickenbacker for the company's troubles.

Finally, in September 1926, an embattled Eddie Rickenbacker issued a message: "Here's where I get off. I can't go along any further because I don't want to be a party to having anyone lose any more money. The **Rickenbacker Company** is in a ditch and out of the race, and the best way I can let people know that we're out of the running is to walk away from the wreck. You'll find my resignation on the table." By November 1926, the company was in receivership. Barney Everitt purchased the Cabot Avenue plant to manufacture aircraft.

Harry Ford Knew that Little Things Mean a Lot

Saxon Motor Company was started by Harry Ford, not Henry. Harry Ford, unrelated to the more famous Ford, believed that a small, two-passenger auto that sold for less than $400 would be popular with the public. In 1913, Harry Ford met Hugh Chalmers while both were working at the National Cash Register Company and convinced him, with ten others, to invest in a company to make the envisioned car.

Harry Ford leased the factory at 1305 Bellevue that had been used for the Demotcar. The **Demotcar Company** had started in 1909 to produce a two-seat runabout that sold for $550; however, it went bankrupt in 1910. The factory was a three-story, fifty-thousand-square-foot building. The first Saxon cars were lightweight, easily maintained vehicles and well received. This style of auto was referred to as a "cyclecar," which was a small, two-passenger vehicle thought to be between a motorcycle and motorcar. For 1915 and 1916, the Saxon was ranked number eight in the nation for auto sales, which led Harry Ford to buy out Hugh Chalmer's stock in the company.

The Saxon couldn't keep up with the Model T of Henry Ford, who had poured millions into his new Highland Park plant on Woodward Avenue and Seven Mile Road in Detroit. Saxon production was moved into a larger facility at 107 Waterloo Street in Detroit formerly used to make the Abbott automobile—a luxury four- or six-cylinder auto produced by the **Abbott-**

The **Saxon Motor Company**'s Bellevue Street factory as it looks in 2015. The Demotcar and Little Princess autos were also assembled here. *Photo by the author.*

Detroit Company from 1909 to 1918. The company briefly moved to Cleveland before going bankrupt. Saxon production could never get the car to the point where it was profitable. When the Waterloo Street factory burned down during World War I and founder Harry Ford succumbed to the influenza epidemic of 1918, Saxon production stopped.

The company was reorganized by C.A. Pfeiffer, new company president, in 1919. By 1922, the factory in Ypsilanti, Michigan, that had manufactured the ACE motorcar was secured to resume production, but by 1923 the company was bankrupt. The ACE was a four-cylinder car built by the **Apex Motor Corporation** in Ypsilanti from 1920 to 1923.

The cyclecar, of which the Saxon was probably the most successful, was one of many utilizing that style of motorcar. Another cyclecar was the Cricket, which was designed in London, England, and brought to Detroit to manufacture. The **Cricket Cyclecar Company** was started and a factory secured at 80 Walker Street in 1913. It was claimed that the Cricket had half as many parts as other autos. Only a few Crickets were manufactured, and in 1914, the company was absorbed by the **Motor Products Company**. Plans called for production to continue but were halted due to the collapse of the cyclecar market.

A similar fate befell the **Princess Cycle Car Company**, at some point renamed the **Princess Motor Car Company**, which announced the release of a cyclecar called the Little Princess. The vehicle had an air-cooled, four-cylinder engine and was first manufactured in a small plant at 348 Clay in Detroit. The small size of the plant and a fire at that location forced the company to relocate to 1305 Bellevue, the former factory of the Demotcar and Saxon. Production continued until January 1919, when it was reported by the trade magazine *Motor Age* that the company was "permanently out of business."

5

DETROIT AREA MOTORCAR COMPANIES

The 1890s was when the first motorcar companies began to raise financing and manufacture autos in the United States. Although all roads eventually led to Detroit when it came to automobile manufacturing, Cleveland and Indianapolis—as well as the rest of Ohio and Indiana—had many early auto companies. Other cities in Michigan besides Detroit had early car companies. These included Flint, Kalamazoo, Marysville, Pontiac, Port Huron and Ypsilanti.

ELWOOD HAYNES

From Metallurgist to Auto Company Mogul

Elwood Haynes (1857–1925) was born in Portland, Indiana, and built his first vehicle at the age of twelve out of scrap railroad parts. He operated it on the county railroad tracks. When the railroad foreman found out, he seized and destroyed the vehicle.

Elwood Haynes was a metallurgist and invented a small vapor thermostat to measure natural gas. He also made significant gains in stainless steel. He built his first gasoline-powered vehicle in 1894, which is believed to be the second American one, after the Charles Duryea motorized wagon. Haynes also made improvements in the rotary gas valve engine.

In 1894, Elwood Haynes partnered with brothers Elmer and Edgar Apperson of Kokomo, Indiana, and built a gasoline-powered automobile. After test-driving the vehicle on July 4, 1894, they formed the **Haynes-Apperson Automobile Company** and began assembling and selling autos.

By 1895, the **Haynes-Apperson Automobile Company** was manufacturing an auto every two to three weeks and selling them for $2,000 apiece. The company ran some endurance races with the auto and gained a lot of favorable publicity. The **Haynes-Apperson Automobile Company** moved to a larger factory and manufactured two more models in 1899. By 1899, the factory was running twenty-four hours a day to keep up with demand.

In 1901, the Apperson brothers and Elwood Haynes parted ways, and the company was renamed the **Haynes Automobile Company**. In 1913, the company manufactured its first V-6 cylinder engine. By 1916, it had a V-12 cylinder engine, which remained in production until 1922, although the company's mainstay was still the six-cylinder engine car models.

The Appersons then went on to form their own company, the Apperson Automobile Company, and manufactured a two-cylinder auto in 1902. In 1903, the brothers increased to a four-cylinder engine, and then in 1908, they manufactured their first six-cylinder auto. The company, which named two of its speedy six-cylinder models Jack Rabbit and Roadaplane, averaged two thousand cars a year until its demise in 1926.

Elwood Haynes was a very early auto pioneer—he had a factory by 1895 producing one or two autos per week. *Author's collection.*

Although the **Duryea Motor Wagon Company** was actually the first, the **Haynes Automobile Company** got a lot of mileage out of claiming to be the first auto company. It manufactured autos until 1924, when business soured. A bankruptcy filing followed, but the company had recovered enough in 1925 to manufacture a few more autos. However, Elwood Haynes died of pneumonia later the same year, and that brought about the ultimate end to America's "first auto company." Many of the Haynes auto plants were repurposed by other auto businesses and are still extant in Kokomo, Indiana. The Smithsonian Institution's National Museum of American History has an 1894 Haynes on permanent exhibit.

Take a Checker Cab to Kalamazoo

The **Partin Manufacturing Company** of Chicago and the **Palmer Motor Car Company** of Detroit joined to form the **Partin-Palmer Motor Car Company** in 1913. Its plan to produce three cars was downsized to just one car, the Partin-Palmer. The second proposed car was a cyclecar called the Pioneer, and the third was referred to as the Partin. After assembling a few cars in Detroit, operations were moved to Chicago by 1914. In 1915, the company built a small twenty-horsepower roadster that sold for $495. It also produced an eight-cylinder model. Unfortunately, neither model sold well, and the company went into bankruptcy.

Commonwealth Motors Corporation took over from its predecessor **Partin-Palmer Motor Car Company**, which was reorganizing after its bankruptcy in 1916. The car, which was originally called the Partin-Palmer, was changed to the Commonwealth. It had a strong frame, built with a solid nickel/steel alloy, and a four-cylinder Lycoming engine. The company merged with **Markin Body Corporation** in 1921 to fulfill a **Checker Cab** contract. The company morphed into the **Checker Motors Corporation** when Morris Markin purchased the **Checker Taxi Company**.

The **Checker Motors Corporation** operated out of Kalamazoo, Michigan, building durable vehicles with large rear seats and trunks. It was established in 1922 and owned by Morris Markin. He purchased the Handley-Knight chassis plant and the Dort body plant in Kalamazoo to build his cabs. The taxicab vehicles came in black, maroon, yellow or "canary."

In 1958, **Checker** put out a consumer passenger car called the Checker Superba. By 1962, three thousand of the consumer vehicles had been sold, but the numbers never went above 20 percent of the company's output, and the other 80 percent was still taxicabs. In addition, **Checker** produced truck bodies for **Hudson**, **Ford** and **REO** in the late 1930s.

The **Checker Motors Corporation** continued building passenger cars and taxicabs and survived antitrust charges in 1964, as well as the death of its founder, Morris Markin, in 1970. The company continued producing autos and taxicabs as it was reorganized in the 1980s. The **Checker Motors Corporation** also supplied parts to **GM**.

In 2008, it suffered lower sales as the recession of 2008 hit, and **GM** went into bankruptcy. Major stockholder Morris Markin's son David Markin fell victim to the Bernie Madoff Ponzi scheme. In 2009, the **Checker Motors Corporation** declared bankruptcy and its assets were sold. In 2010, the sale of the Kalamazoo headquarters signaled the end for this venerable American company.

From Carriages to the American Rolls-Royce

McFarlan Car Company

Another Indiana auto company was the **McFarlan Carriage Company** of Connersville. The business was started in 1841 by John B. McFarlan, who concentrated on always improving his product. Over the years, the **McFarlan Carriage Company** won prizes for the high quality of its buggies and carriages.

The company had been in business for more than fifty years by 1909, when the grandson of the founder, Alfred Harry McFarlan, began using the company name and resources to build "motor buggies." It was evident that these would be more than just horse buggies as the new company name was announced—**McFarlan Car Company**. McFarlan and the company directors decided that only six-cylinder cars would be built—contrary to the usual four-cylinder models of the day. The motto reflected it—"Builders of Six Cylinder Cars Exclusively." The McFarlan was priced in the middle of most cars of the day—averaging about $2,100 per car.

In 1912, gasoline-powered cars became self-starting, not requiring cranking to start. This feature was a great boon since cranking the car to start it was what kept most women from driving cars.

1925 McFARLANE, owned by Jack Dempsey on display at Movie World, Buena Park, California.

As the caption reads, this 1925 McFarlan belonged to champion boxer Jack Dempsey. (The caption incorrectly puts an "e" on McFarlan.) *Author's collection.*

The 1920s saw the McFarlan autos get longer and wider, and they were even dubbed "the American Rolls-Royce." Customers included celebrities Mary Pickford, Paul Whiteman, Fatty Arbuckle, Wallace Reid, Jack Dempsey and Al Capone—who bought two, one for him and one for his wife. The company hit some rough patches and didn't recover. The **McFarlan Car Company** went into bankruptcy in 1928.

"It's a Doozy" in Connersville

And a Cord and Auburn Too

Remarkably, the McFarlan wasn't the only car built in the small town of Connersville, Indiana, population thirteen thousand. In fact, a number of luxury cars were built there. The Auburn, Cord, Duesenberg and others were all associated with Connersville, the only city in Fayette County, Indiana.

One manufacturer that ended up in Connersville was the **Auburn Automobile Company**. It started in Auburn, Indiana, with Charles Eckhart and two of his sons, Frank and Morris, in 1900. Similar to the McFarlans, the Eckharts started in the carriage industry. Frank was the salesperson for the **Eckhart Carriage Company**, and when he was on the road making sales calls, he saw and purchased a Curved Dash Oldsmobile in Lansing, Michigan. Frank, Morris and Charles Eckhart experimented and came up with their own automobile. Their first cars were one-cylinder, chain-driven runabouts. In 1905, they started using a two-cylinder engine, and in 1912, they changed to a six-cylinder.

In 1919, the Eckharts sold the business to a Chicago group of businessmen, including William Wrigley Jr. of the chewing gum empire. The factory continued building cars and, in 1912, introduced a six-cylinder auto. In 1924, Errett Lobban Cord became general manager of the company and, in 1925, introduced new models with eight-cylinder engines. With stylish nickel plating and two-tone coloring, Cord doubled sales three years in a row. The offerings expanded to include speedsters, phaetons, roadsters, touring cars, runabouts and town coupe models.

The **Duesenberg Motor Company** was founded by Fred Duesenberg in Indianapolis, Indiana, in 1920. With his brother August, he created one of the most loved of American automobiles. The catchphrase "It's a doozy" (or "duesy") originally referred to the Duesenberg. Known at first

As the slogan on the display window says, the Duesenberg was "built to outclass, outrun, and outlast any car on the road." *Author's collection.*

as a winning race car, the production of Duesenbergs started in 1920 and lasted until 1937.

In 1926, Errett Cord became president of the **Auburn Automobile Company**, and a vast distribution network was set up. With the company doing so well, in 1929, the **Auburn Automobile Company** acquired **Lexington Motor Company** and the **Duesenberg Motor Company**, as well as **Anstead Engine Company**, **Lycoming Engine**, **Limousine Body** and **Central Manufacturing**.

The **Anstead Engine Company** had larger facilities in Connersville than the Auburn's present location there, so production for the **Auburn Automobile Company** was transferred to Anstead's factory in 1926. The **Auburn Automobile Company** survived the 1929 stock market crash and introduced the Cord, a front-wheel-drive luxury car. Although it was known for its front-wheel drive, the Cord was also the first car to have hidden headlights.

The **Lexington Motor Company** was started in Lexington, Kentucky, in 1909 by race horse promoter Knisey Stone. The company was enticed to move into and share the **McFarlan Car Company** factories at 1950 Columbia Street in Connersville, Indiana. Engineer John C. Moore developed the first dual-exhaust system for this car, called the Lexington. The Lexington Minute Man Six was marketed with the slogan "Like a machine gun that does not choke." In 1913, the company was acquired by E.W. Anstead to assemble his car called the Howard.

The recession following World War I took its toll on the company. In 1922, production plummeted to one-third of what it had been the year before. In 1927, the **Lexington Motor Company** was purchased by the **Auburn Automobile Company**. The brand name of the Lexington was retired as the last Lexingtons were marketed under the **Anstead** name in 1926 and 1927.

When Errett Cord sold his interest in the company in 1937, the Auburn, Cord and Duesenberg nameplates were discontinued. Cord had gotten into aircraft manufacturing and shipbuilding and had been having problems with the Internal Revenue Service and the Securities and Exchange Commission.

The **Rider Lewis Motorcar Company** started in Anderson, Indiana, in 1908. It produced $1,000 cars in 1908 and 1909 and then was purchased by Henry Nyberg of Chicago, Illinois, in 1910. The car produced was the Nyberg, which was handmade until the company went out of business in 1914.

The **Model Automobile Company** was founded in Peru, Indiana, in 1902 by attorney E.A. Myers. He bought out a machine shop in Auburn and started manufacturing engines and, in 1904, a gasoline-powered automobile. In 1906, he moved the operation to Peru and manufactured more than three hundred autos, called the Model, with touring and runabout models. By 1907, Myers was running a parts division and separated the **Model Gas Engine Works** from the parts division before selling it. He named the auto company the **Great Western Automobile Company**. As **Great Western**, he produced six-cylinder autos until 1916, when the company went out of business.

Indianapolis is the home of the Indianapolis 500, or the "Indy 500," one of the most famous auto races. It is a five-hundred-mile race that began in 1911 and is held in Indianapolis every year on Memorial Day. It's therefore fitting that Indianapolis was also the home of a number of automobile and auto parts companies. A ten-block area on North Capitol Street was dubbed "Auto Row."

The Indianapolis 500 track is pictured in the 1920s. Winning the Indy 500 was certain to help auto sales. *Author's collection.*

The Stutz Bearcat originally was priced in the $2,000 range and today is much prized by collectors and sells for more than $300,000. *Photo by the author.*

In 1911, the **Stutz Motor Car Company of America, Inc.** began in Indianapolis as a luxury car manufacturer. Originally called the **Ideal Car Company**, the founder, Harry C. Stutz, began making high-performance roadsters in a factory at 1002 North Capitol Avenue after entering a car in the Indianapolis 500 in 1911. The Stutz Bearcat was the most famous of the Stutz cars. The company also produced the Blackhawk, a less expensive Stutz, from 1928 until 1930, when it was discontinued due to the onset of the Great Depression. The **Stutz Motor Car Company** stopped production in 1935.

WILLYS-OVERLAND BECOMES A MAJOR PLAYER

The first car of the **Overland Auto Works** Company was a runabout constructed by Claude Cox while he was employed by the **Standard Wheel Company** of Terre Haute, Indiana, in 1903. **Standard Wheel** allowed Cox to relocate to Indianapolis to manufacture his car in 1905. Cox manufactured cars for three years, and then the company was purchased by John North Willys. In 1912, the company was renamed **Willys-Overland Motor Company**. From 1912 to 1918, the company was number two in U.S. auto sales, behind only **Ford**.

In 1916, **Willys** purchased the **Russell Motor Car Company** of Toronto, Ontario, the first successful auto company in Canada. In 1919, the company acquired the old **Duesenberg** plant in Elizabeth, New Jersey. In the mid-1920s, **Willys** purchased the **F.B. Stearns Company** of Cleveland, Ohio, and continued to produce the successful Stearns-Knight luxury car.

Willys planned to build a new, larger plant in 1920 but was hit hard by the recession that year. Walter P. Chrysler, who was hired to manage the company, scrapped the planned Willys Six for a new car called the Chrysler Six. The Elizabeth, New Jersey plant and the Chrysler Six prototype were both sold to Billy Durant, who was forming his third auto conglomerate, **Durant Motors**. His first had been **GM**, and his second was the **United Motors Company**. Chrysler moved on to manufacture the Chrysler Six at **Maxwell Motor Company**, which, in 1925, became the **Chrysler Corporation**.

The Overland continued to be manufactured until 1926, when the car was replaced by a smaller vehicle called the Willys Whippet. During the

The **Overland Auto Works** factory of Toledo, Ohio, became part of the **Willys Company** in 1908. From 1912 to 1918, it was second only to the **Ford Motor Company** in overall auto sales. *Author's collection.*

Depression, a number of brands were discontinued—the Stearns-Knight in 1929, the Whippet in 1931 and the Willys-Knight in 1933. Production instead continued on the Willys Six and Willys Eight.

The company continued to reorganize and, in 1936, produced the Willys 77. In 1939, Bendix hydraulic brakes were featured and horsepower was upped from forty-eight horsepower to sixty-one horsepower.

In 1938, Joseph Frazer became the head of **Willys** and engineered the awarding of the contract to build Jeeps, a military concept car designed by Byron Q. Jones, to the **Willys Company**. Work commenced in 1941 and continued throughout World War II. After the war, **Willys** did not restart production on its other cars but continued building the Jeep.

Willys entered the passenger car market again with the Willys Aero in 1952. It was a six-cylinder, two-door sedan model. In 1953, a four-door sedan and a two-door hardtop model were added, and **Kaiser Motor Company** purchased **Willys**. The new company produced Aeros for two more years and then concentrated on Jeeps. In 1963, the company name became **Kaiser-Jeep Corporation**. It was purchased by the **American Motors Company** in 1970.

In 1904, Joseph J. Cole purchased the **Gates-Osborne Carriage Company** of Indianapolis and renamed it the **Cole Carriage Company**.

The Overland auto was designed by Claude Cox and manufactured until 1926. *Author's collection.*

In 1908, the enterprising Joseph Cole invented a horseless carriage he called the Cole Solid Tire Automobile. The vehicle was of the "highwheeler" type, styled like a horse carriage with an engine. It wasn't until Cole took it out for its first test drive that he realized he hadn't installed any kind of brake system. His solution was to drive in circles around the Soldiers' and Sailors' Monument in Indianapolis until he ran out of gas.

The brake problem was rectified, and Cole sold 170 vehicles. In 1905, he decided that the highwheeler style was not the best style for a motorized vehicle. He reorganized as the **Cole Motor Company**, and his next product was a more traditional sedan style offered with either a two- or four-cylinder engine. At the end of 1910, he had sold 783 vehicles, enough to keep producing cars and show a profit.

The Cole Model 30 won many racing contests, including the Vanderbilt Cup in 1910, and it evolved into a luxury vehicle whose main competition was the Cadillac. The 1913 version offered a six-cylinder engine, electric starting and lights. In 1915, the V-8 engine replaced all the four- and six- cylinder types. Some of the later imperious-sounding model names were Cole Equipages, Sportosine, Tourosine, Tuxedo Foursome and Ultra-Sportster. J.J. Cole's company reached its peak in

1919 when it produced 6,225 cars. In 1920, most of the car companies suffered shortages of metal and other car materials. When Cole started losing money in the early 1920s, he decided to liquidate the company, which he completed by 1925.

The **Marion Automobile Company** started at 321–41 West Fifteenth Street in Indianapolis, and in 1904, it started building an air-cooled, sixteen-horsepower, four-cylinder auto. It was later water cooled. The company produced famous twelve-cylinder race cars known as the Bobcat and the Comet. Perpetually undercapitalized, it was taken over by the machinations of J.J. Handley in 1912. In 1914, Handley also acquired the **Imperial Motor Company** and formed the **Mutual Motors Company**. He then moved the entire operation to Jackson, Michigan.

The **Marmon Motor Car Company** was founded by Howard Marmon in Indianapolis in 1902. The parent company, **Nordyke Marmon & Company**, started manufacturing flour-grinding mill equipment in 1851. The company's first autos in 1902 were of an experimental type, with an air-cooled, V-twin engine. Over subsequent years, the company brought out four- and eight-cylinder autos with the name of Marmon.

In 1909, the popular **Marmon Motor Car Company** car called the Wasp came out. It won the very first Indy 500 in 1911. The 1913 Model 48 had a six-cylinder gasoline engine, electric headlights, a horn and electric courtesy lights for the dashboard and doors. Like many cars of the day, the Wasp came with a tool kit. The Marmon kit included a power tire pump, jack, chassis oiler, tire patch kit and flashlight. **Marmon Motor Car Company** also introduced the rear view mirror on autos.

Marmon Motor Car Company produced the Roosevelt in 1929 and 1930, an eight-cylinder auto offered in sedan or coupe for less than $1,000. It was named for President Theodore Roosevelt. In 1931, **Marmon** introduced its V-12 engine and changed the name of the Roosevelt to the Marmon 16. It stopped making automobiles in 1933, the worst year of the Great Depression. Instead, it teamed up with engineer Colonel Arthur Herrington to make all-wheel-drive vehicles and trucks. The new company was called the **Marmon-Herrington Company** and was eventually absorbed by Berkshire Hatheway.

The **National Motor Vehicle Company** made cars at 1101–47 East Twenty-second Street in Indianapolis from 1900 to 1924. At first a producer of electric vehicles from 1901 to 1908, the company started manufacturing gasoline-powered vehicles in 1905. In 1922, the company entered into a merger with the **Jackson Motor Company** and the company that made the Dixie Flyer, the **Kentucky Wagon Manufacturing Company**, to become the **Associated Motor Car Company**. This company lasted only until 1924.

The **Parry Motor Company** was located at 1002 West Henry Street in Indianapolis and produced autos named the Parry and the New Parry from 1910 until 1912. David MacLean Parry got into the auto business when he gained control of the **Overland** company. He sold out in 1907 but then started the **Parry Motor Company** in 1909. The company produced the Parry in 1910 in seven large, leased buildings with 386 employees. Slow sales (only nine hundred cars sold) did not stop the company from bringing out the New Parry in 1911.

In 1912, David Parry changed the name of the company to the **Motor Car Manufacturing Company** and put out an auto called the Pathfinder. For a while, both the New Parry and the Pathfinder were built in the same factory. However, the restructuring was too late; the company had overextended itself too much and went into receivership. By the end of 1912, it was gone.

The **Premier Motor Manufacturing Company** was started in 1903 by George A. Weidely and Harold O. Smith. The company produced touring cars with air-cooled engines in Indianapolis until 1928, when it was sold to **National Cab and Truck Company** of Indianapolis.

In Lafayette, Indiana, the **American Motor Vehicle Company** produced two cars from 1916 to 1920, including the American Junior. The Junior was marketed to children but supposedly was suited for adults and cost $160. The other car produced by the company was for adults, although you wouldn't know it from the name of the car—Auto Red Bug. This car was a "buckboard," which was a four-wheel wagon of simple construction. It was designed in 1916 and sold to **A.O. Smith Company**, which marketed it as the Smith Flyer. The **American Motor Vehicle Company** made another try at the small auto market with a $360, two-person roadster marketed to adults. However, because it was so well-known as a maker of children's cars, it was hard for adults to take the company seriously, and it was out of business by 1920.

John William Lambert was one of the pioneers of the auto industry and was considered by many to be the inventor of the first gasoline-powered vehicles, which he introduced in 1891. Called the Buckeye Gasoline Buggy, it featured the friction gearing disk drive transmission that Lambert developed. Although he offered to hand make the auto for clients, he had no takers. So in 1892, he started the **Lambert Gas and Gasoline Engine Company** and the **Buckeye Manufacturing Company** to make gasoline engines and farm implements.

Lambert started the **Union Automobile Company** in Union City, Indiana, and began making automobiles in 1902. The car the company built featured the transmission designed by Lambert. The car was called the Union. **Buckeye Manufacturing Company** manufactured the car motors. The car was a two-seater with a folding collapsible front seat to accommodate two more passengers. The second year's model was much like the first but with the motor placed in the rear of the car.

In 1905, the auto company moved to Third and Sycamore Streets in Anderson, Indiana, and the name of the car was changed to the Lambert. From 1905 through 1918, the company manufactured trucks, fire engines and tractors as well as autos. The 1906 Lambert, as well as most Lambert models to follow, was chain-driven rather than shaft-driven. By 1910, the company had more than one thousand employees and produced more than three thousand autos per year until 1916.

The following year the factory converted to war production for World War I and produced military fire engines, ammunition shells and caisson wheels. At the end of the war, the **Union Automobile Company** stopped making complete autos and started focusing on auto parts. Founder John Lambert said that he realized "auto production was best left to the larger companies." The company produced auto parts until 1922, when they got completely out of the auto business.

The **Elcar Carriage Company** manufactured the Elcar car from 1915 to 1931 in Elkhart, Indiana. The carriage company had been in business for thirty years when it started producing cars. It had cars called the Elkhart and the Elcar. The original owners, William B. and George B. Pratt, sold the company to a group of investors in 1921 and the name was changed to the **Elcar Motor Company**.

In 1930, the **Elcar Motor Company** entered into a contract to produce the El-Fay taxi for Larry Fay. Fay was an infamous New York rumrunner with forty-nine arrests but no felony convictions who brought whiskey in from Canada to New York. With his profits, he bought a nightclub and a taxicab company. The taxis were built by the **Elcar Motor Company** until New Year's Eve 1932, when Larry Fay was killed instantly by four slugs to the head and heart. Fay was shot by a disgruntled doorman at his nightclub who had just been informed his pay was being lowered.

Hit by the Great Depression and Fay's death, the **Elcar Motor Company** entered bankruptcy in 1933. The **Allied Cab Manufacturing**

Company used the **Elcar Motor Company** factory to manufacture taxicabs from 1932 to 1935, and the **Crow Motor Company** produced an auto called the Black Crow from 1909 until 1911, also in Elkhart, Indiana.

The **Pilot Motor Car Company** was owned by George Seidel, who also owned the **Seidel Buggy Company** in Richmond, Indiana. The car was called a Pilot and was initially built in the factory of the buggy company until its own factory was built across the street. Initially, the cars had a four-cylinder engine. In 1913, it was switched to a six-cylinder engine. The **Pilot Motor Car Company** took over the **Lorraine Motors Corporation** in 1924 and produced a few hearses under the Lorraine name before the **Pilot Motor Car Company** was forced into receivership. By 1925, the company was defunct, and the factory was sold for $28,500.

Richmond, Indiana, was also home to two different companies that each manufactured a car named the Richmond. The **Richmond Automobile Company** manufactured a two-cylinder steam vehicle that weighed just forty-eight pounds. This car, called the Richmond, was built from 1902 to 1903.

The other Richmond was built by **Wayne Works**, a farming tool manufacturer since the 1870s. In 1901, company president Walter Schultz told Jack St. John to design a car "because everyone else is." This car was, at first, a two-cylinder touring car, although the next year, a four-cylinder engine was offered. It was well-regarded for its reliability and its hill-climbing capability.

Richmond, Indiana, wasn't done yet. The **George W. Davis Motor Car Company** made a car called the Davis in Richmond from 1908 to 1929. The company made a few motorized buggies from 1908 until 1910, and in 1911, it had a touring car with a four-cylinder engine. Later, a six-cylinder was offered before the company folded in 1929.

Winton Drives His "Automobile" from Cleveland to New York

From the late 1890s to the early 1900s, the leading automotive city was Cleveland, Ohio. With easy access to glass, steel and rubber, Cleveland retained the number two position even after Detroit became the undisputed Motor City. Leading the Cleveland pack was car pioneer Alexander Winton.

Before Scotsman Alexander Winton, who owned a bicycle shop, started assembling a standard automobile model in 1896, auto companies would customize each automobile to the customer's specifications. Winton assembled the same standard auto each time, starting a precedent in the industry. The **Winton Motor Company** was the first to construct "ready-made" cars, as opposed to "custom made."

In 1897, Winton drove one of his cars, named the Winton, from Cleveland to New York City, an eight-hundred-mile trip. When this feat did not receive much media attention, he repeated it and made sure he had the attention of the newspapers by having the *Cleveland Plain Dealer* newspaper sponsor the trip. He was accompanied by *Plain Dealer* reporter Charlie Shanks, who is credited with popularizing the French phrase "automobile" for the vehicle they were riding in. On this second trip, Winton was met by more than one million people when he arrived in New York. The trip did much to popularize the automobile. In 1903, a Winton was driven from San Francisco to New York, the first transcontinental auto trip.

The **Winton Company** was a pioneer in the auto field until 1924, when Winton dissolved the company. Before that happened, he had one unhappy customer try to tell him how to improve his vehicles. Alex Winton said something along the lines of, "If you know so much, why don't you make your own car?" The customer was James L. Packard, who replied that

The 1906 Winton is pictured. The 1897 Winton was driven eight hundred miles from Cleveland to New York City, which provided excellent publicity for the fledgling automobile. *Author's collection.*

maybe he would. He later went on to found his own company, the **Packard Motor Car Company**, which made luxury cars for more than fifty years.

Winton wasn't the only one to bring luster to Cleveland's auto history. The **Hansen Automobile Company** brought out cars named the Cleveland and sometimes the Hansen. Rasmus Hansen designed a single-cylinder, six-horsepower car in 1902 and, later, a car called the General. A company known as the **Cleveland Motor Car Company** also had cars named the Cleveland and the Cleveland Roadster. By 1907, all these Cleveland companies had called it quits, perhaps because they couldn't keep track of all the cars named the Cleveland.

The **Chandler Motor Company** was formed by Frederick C. Chandler and four other partners in 1913. By 1915, the company produced seven thousand of its brand name car, the Chandler, a good, dependable, midrange-priced vehicle. Production more than doubled to fifteen thousand autos the following year. After World War I ended, the company realized it would need a small auto for the returning troops. Thus, yet another of the cars named the Cleveland was manufactured, and the company was renamed the **Chandler-Cleveland Motor Company**. In 1920, it had a line of six models. Its peak year was 1927, when sales exceeded twenty thousand cars.

ASK THE BILLIONAIRE WHO DRIVES ONE

Peerless Had No Peers

The **Peerless Motor Company** of Cleveland, Ohio, produced one of the "Three P's" of luxury brands, the other two being the **Pierce-Arrow** and the **Packard**. The **Peerless Motor Company** autos, first manufactured in 1900, introduced drum brakes to the industry and the standard of having a front-mounted engine driving the rear wheels through a shaft.

The **Peerless** brand started in 1902 and was popularized in 1904 with the Green Dragon, driven by famed race-car driver Barney Oldfield, who set multiple world speed records. From 1905 through 1907, the **Peerless** brand became a more luxurious brand and was purchased by J.D. Rockefeller and Cornelius Vanderbilt.

Peerless introduced its V-8 engine in 1915 and was one of the first autos to incorporate electric lights. During World War I, **Peerless** produced military vehicles and after the war returned to luxury vehicle production. In 1929, the Peerless was successfully redesigned to compete with the Marmon and Stutz Bearcat autos. However, the end wasn't far away, as the Great Depression began to minimize the amount of people who could afford a luxury car. **Peerless** attempted to stay alive by marketing a stripped-down version of its car, but its last model, with a V-16 engine, came out in 1931. The **Peerless Motor Company** remained idle until 1933, when Prohibition was repealed. The company revamped its factory to produce Carling Black Label and Red Cap beer.

When the auto industry was centered in Cleveland in the early 1900s, it evolved from having each company construct its own parts to separate companies specializing in making one type of part, such as manifolds. As Detroit increased in prominence as the manufacturing hub for autos, Cleveland became an auto parts manufacturing city, with many separate companies concentrating on various components for the auto world.

NEWSPAPER PUBLISHER SWITCHES TO AUTO PRODUCTION AND WINS WITH THE WINTON

The **Franklin Automobile Company** manufactured automobiles in Syracuse, New York, from 1902 until 1934. Starting as the **H.H. Franklin Manufacturing Company** in 1893, owner Herbert H. Franklin was a former newspaper publisher who was manufacturing die castings in 1901. When he met inventor John Wilkinson and took a ride in a car Wilkinson had developed for the **New York Automobile Company**, Franklin decided to produce automobiles. The **New York Automobile Company** that hired Wilkinson to develop prototypes neglected to pay him, so Wilkinson felt justified letting Franklin have the auto designs. When the **New York Automobile Company** sued H.H. Franklin for the designs, Franklin ended up absorbing the company.

The new car was called the Franklin and was a four-cylinder runabout with the air-cooled engine developed by Wilkinson in 1901. In 1902, Franklin started manufacturing the autos in his Syracuse factory and was one of the top-five auto producers in the nation from 1905 to 1908. Although those were the company's top years, the **H.H. Franklin Manufacturing Company** stayed in business making autos until 1934.

In 1913, the first sedan style was introduced, one which the Syracuse company would thereafter adopt for all its cars. High quality with less weight was a guiding principle for the Franklin auto, and improvements to

The **Franklin Automobile Company** was one of the longest-operating independent auto companies, in business from 1904 until 1934. *Photo by the author.*

the engineering and frame continued throughout the years. The Franklin won speed and endurance contests and set a record at 40.3 miles per gallon.

Even though the Franklin was considered a quality car, in 1923, the dealers descended on Syracuse, demanding a new look to the car or they would drop their franchises. This upset Wilkinson, who quit and went to work for **Dodge Brothers**, developing its "Victory Six" engine. In 1917, during World War I, Wilkinson helped develop the Liberty V-12, a 450-horsepower aircraft engine.

The **Franklin Automobile Company** made the changes the dealers demanded, and a new style was introduced as Franklin Series II in 1925. The first use of front-wheel brakes was in 1928 with the Airman, named for aviator Charles Lindbergh, who drove Franklins. Because of the stock market crash in 1929, sales and production dwindled. The **Franklin Automobile Company** was a victim of the Great Depression, going out of business in 1934.

The Dodge Brothers Build Cars and Wreak Havoc

Horace Elgin Dodge and John Francis Dodge, better known as the **Dodge Brothers**, were born in a wooden cottage in Niles, Michigan, in 1864 and 1868, respectively. They both began working in a machine shop established by their grandfather, where they learned about marine engines.

After developing their skills in the family shop, the brothers moved on to the Detroit-based Murphy Engine Company in 1886 and then to the Canadian Typograph Company in nearby Windsor, Ontario, in 1890. Horace secured a patent for adjustable ball bearing bicycle hubs, and in 1897, the brothers entered into a partnership with Fred S. Evans to produce **Dodge and Evans Bicycles**.

The Dodge brothers sold the bicycle business in 1901 and returned from Windsor to Detroit, where they opened a shop building transmissions and engines for **Olds Motor Works**. The machine shop was at 133–37 Beaubien Street in the Boydell Building. A September 1901 article in the *Detroit Free Press* praised the business as "one of the most thoroughly equipped and up-to-date in the city."

The Boydell Building in the Greektown district of Detroit looks much the same as when it housed the **Dodge Brothers** business in 1901. *Photo by the author.*

Dodge Bros. Automobile Plant, Detroit, Mich.

The **Dodge Brothers** factory, located on Joseph Campau Street in Detroit, was one of the largest auto plants in its day. *Author's collection.*

In 1902, the Dodge brothers opened a larger shop at the corner of Monroe Street and Hastings Street in Detroit and employed more than two hundred men. In 1903, they agreed to become a major supplier of auto components to the **Ford Motor Company**. The components consisted of the "engine, transmission, and axles, mounted on a frame." The first agreement called for 650 units. By accepting **Ford** stock as payment, the brothers quickly saw their money accumulate. As the **Ford Motor Company**'s fortunes rose, so did those of the Dodge brothers. By 1910, they had a factory complex in Hamtramck, a small city surrounded by Detroit.

Times were good, but as Henry Ford headed toward self-sufficiency, with the **Ford Motor Company** making more of its own components, the Dodge brothers decided the time was right to produce their own auto. Their first car, the Dodge Model 30, was designed by Horace Dodge and constructed in 1914. The **Dodge Brothers Motor Company** name and good reputation for quality helped create strong sales.

The Dodge auto became known for its all-steel body at a time when most autos were mostly wood. Although the Hupmobile was actually the first all-steel body, the Dodge brothers successfully used the boast in their advertising. In 1915, they manufactured forty-five thousand **Dodge Brothers** cars. By 1916, the **Dodge Brothers** passenger auto was in second place in sales

(**Ford** was in first place) and would remain there for the next four years. Overall, the **Dodge Brothers** were in the top four in U.S. sales from 1916 until 1926—years after the founders had passed.

The **Dodge Brothers** were known to be popular among dealers, not requiring them to pay for unsold stock. When a parts shortage following World War I caused less production and therefore fewer sales for Dodge dealers, only one dealer went out of business. And when production went back up, the factories couldn't keep up with the amount of Dodges the dealers were selling.

John and Horace Dodge were known as hell-raisers, and there are many incidents that reflect their late-night drunken escapades. One story is how John Dodge forced a saloon owner to dance on the top of his bar by threatening him with a pistol. Dodge expressed his admiration for the dancing by throwing glasses at and breaking the mirror over the bar. Another incident had John Dodge punching an editor of the *Detroit Times* newspaper when the editor criticized a friend of Dodge's in print. Horace also had his violent moments, such as the cold night when his car wouldn't start and a passerby made a snide comment. Horace responded by punching him in the nose.

The Dodge brothers contributed greatly to charitable causes, such as Orchestra Hall and the Detroit Symphony Orchestra, and were also admired and well liked due to their upright treatment of their employees. It was only because of these charitable acts that they were accepted by a reluctant Detroit upper-class society, which was not well-disposed to see the often alcohol-fueled Dodge brothers at their cultured events.

If the Grosse Pointe Country Club refused to accept his family, Horace Dodge said, he would build a palace next door to the club's establishment that would make it "look like a shanty" in comparison. It did refuse him, and he built a red sandstone English Renaissance–style dwelling (containing a huge, world-famous pipe organ) that indeed made the Grosse Pointe Country Club look shanty-like in comparison.

Sometimes, the Dodge brothers would trash the bar they were in and then tell the owner to just send them the bill. Both brothers were millionaires many times over by this time. However, they conducted their most destructive drunken escapades in the more rundown bars, maybe to keep expenses down.

Perhaps their bar antics are why they took a light approach to alcohol at work, allowing men to drink beer inside of the factory, knowing it kept them from wandering away and not working. This practice was curtailed when broken beer bottles were discovered in malfunctioning machines.

Sadly, both brothers died of influenza in 1920. Some accounts give Howard's cause of death as cirrhosis. Their large mausoleum in Detroit's Woodlawn Cemetery is well known for its Egyptian sculptures and theme. Nearby the Dodge brothers' mausoleum are other car company namesakes. The Grinnell mausoleum of the **Grinnell Electric Car Company** and the Grinnell Brothers Piano Company is next to the Dodges' and next to that is J.L. Hudson, who the **Hudson Motor Car Company** was named for. In between the Dodges and Grinnells is the grave of C. Harold Wills of the **Wills Ste. Claire Motor Company**.

After the Dodge brothers' deaths, the company continued at the behest of the **Dodge Brothers Company** widows. One of the most notable presidents of the **Dodge Brothers Company** during this period was Frederick Haynes, who entered into a partnership with the Graham brothers (Joseph, Robert and Ray), collectively known as **Graham Brothers, Inc.** They would later become the Graham in the **Graham-Paige Motors Corporation. Graham Brothers, Inc.** was known for producing medium- and heavyweight trucks. The

The Dodge brothers' tomb in Detroit's Woodlawn Cemetery is known for its Egyptian motif. *Photo by the author.*

The **Mason Motor Company** of Indianapolis became the **Maytag-Mason Automobile Company**. *Author's collection.*

Dodge Brothers Company purchased **Graham Brothers, Inc.** and got into the truck business in a big way.

It wasn't until the company dropped out of the auto industry's top four in 1925 that the Dodge widows decided to sell the company to **Dillon, Read & Company** for $146 million—the largest cash transaction to that date. In 1928, **Dillon, Read & Company** sold the company to **Chrysler**. "Brothers" was dropped from the name, but the Dodge brand lives on in trucks and cars for the **Chrysler Corporation**.

The **Mason Motor Company** started in Des Moines, Iowa, in 1909. It was founded by Fred and August Duesenberg and lawyer Edward R. Mason. The car it produced was called the Mason.

Frederick Louis Maytag purchased the company in 1909. More well known for making washing machines, Maytag was one of the many successful businessmen who wanted to have a go at producing automobiles. Renaming the company the **Maytag-Mason Automobile Company**, the auto was renamed the Maytag and came out in 1910. Maytag sold his interest in the company by 1912, and its name went back to **Mason Motor Company**. It went bankrupt in 1915. Maytag went on to greater success producing washing machines.

FROM BIRDCAGES TO MOTORCARS

The Pierce-Arrow

The **Pierce-Arrow Motor Car Company** began in Buffalo, New York, and produced its first car for sale in 1901. The first business of the founding company was making birdcages. The company, which started in 1865, also produced ice boxes and other household items. In 1896, bicycles were growing in popularity, and the company added bikes to its product line. It next brought out a steam car in 1900 that was not successful.

David Ferguson joined the firm as an engineer and supervised the development of the gasoline-powered Pierce-Arrow. A big success, by 1915, the company had produced more than fifteen thousand automobiles. The three most luxurious cars were said to be the Three P's—**Peerless**, **Pierce-Arrow** and **Packard**.

After many illustrious years, the **Pierce-Arrow Motor Car Company** was placed in the receivership of the **Studebaker Corporation** in 1923 due to faltering sales. In 1933, a group of Buffalo businessmen purchased the Pierce-Arrow nameplate from **Studebaker** and produced more Pierce-Arrows until 1938.

The 1906 Pierce Racine Touring Car from the **Pierce-Arrow Motor Car Company** was considered one of the premier luxury cars. *Photo by the author.*

Ford's Right-Hand Man Builds a Better Car While Planning a Model City

Childe Harold Wills (1878–1940) hated the name Childe, so he went by C. Harold Wills his whole life. He was Henry Ford's chief engineer during the **Ford Motor Company**'s formative years and helped bring Ford's automotive ideas to fruition. Wills then went on to form his own luxury auto company, the **Wills Ste. Claire Motor Company**.

Wills was born in 1878 in Fort Wayne, Indiana, where his father worked as a railway mechanic. Eight years later, the Wills family moved to Detroit. Harold attended Detroit public schools and afterward furthered his education by reading trade journals. He first worked at the same place as his father, the Detroit Lubricator Company. He then got work as an engineer at the Boyer Machine Company, which later became the Burroughs Adding Machine Company.

While working at the Boyer Machine Company, Wills became associated with Henry Ford and was soon using his drawing and drafting skills to flesh out Ford's automotive visions. One of his creations was the **Ford** logo still used today. Ford was just forming his first auto company, the **Detroit Automotive Company**, and Wills would spend his off-hours working with Ford in their rented workshop. Together they built Ford's famous race cars, the 999 and the Arrow. These cars would go on to set speed records on the ice of Anchor Bay in New Baltimore, Michigan, in 1904. While working on the cars, their fingers would start to stiffen from the cold. Because the workshop didn't have heat, they would don boxing gloves and box until the circulation in their hands was sufficient for them to resume working on their engines.

While assembling Ford's Quadracycle, Ford and Wills discovered that their new invention would not fit out the door of the workshop, so they had to take an axe and chop through a wooden wall to get it out. The landlord let Ford put a door there after the wall dismantling.

Ford and Wills also worked together on the Model A. Unfortunately, Wills had an accident with the prototype and totaled it while driving down Mack Avenue in Detroit. He was forgiven and worked with Ford for many years after. Other innovations Wills helped with were the assembly line, the four-cylinder engine block with a detachable cylinder head and the transverse leaf-spring suspension used on early **Ford** models.

Wills and Ford had a falling out when the Model T was released. Ford wanted a minimum of changes so as to keep all the parts interchangeable

C. Harold Wills, later to start the **Wills Ste. Claire Motor Company**, worked with Henry Ford in 1902 to build Ford's famous race car, the 999. The car went on to set speed records on Lake St. Clair and help Ford attract backers to form a new auto company. *Author's collection.*

Ford's workshop on 58 Bagley Avenue in Detroit was where Wills helped Ford build the 999 race car. The building was later moved to Greenfield Village, and the original Bagley location is marked by a plaque. *Author's collection.*

while Wills wanted to keep improving the car. When Ford refused to change the Model T, Wills left Ford's employ and took with him a fortune in patents, stock and more. At first, his plans were to build a better car, but his ideas expanded into building a model community in which he would house his workers and build his production facilities. Wills formed a land company and, in 1919, purchased 4,400 acres on the St. Clair River in an area serviced by railroad, road and river transportation. His "city of contented living," as he called it, was later absorbed by Marysville, Michigan, a nearby settlement that began in 1786 with a sawmill built on Bunce Creek.

The model city was to include schools, churches, parks, housing on lots "large enough to have a vegetable garden," playgrounds, a hotel, stores and a bank. Also planned were ten "community houses" to accommodate single men. Each structure was designed for sixty men. (There would later be a "Salt Block" in Marysville composed of housing for the Morton Salt Company, once a large business in the area—so Wills's idea didn't totally go up in smoke.)

Although the town was set up and designed long before, the **Wills Ste. Claire Motor Company** factory wasn't up and running until January 1921, and the first car didn't roll off of the assembly line until that spring. Wills wanted his cars to be as fine an auto as could be built, even if it cost six times as much as the **Ford** Model T, which it did.

By 1922, the car was successful, with a sell-out of the previous year models and a doubling of production for the year to follow. However, by October, the company was in receivership. Using financing from Boston bankers, the company embarked on the next year's models with many improvements.

The **Wills Ste. Claire Motor Company** continued with new models every year up to 1926. By 1927, the company had failed to show a profit, with low production often caused by Wills stopping production while he made improvements. That same year, the company started to decline and, by the end of the year, was only making custom autos with parts on hand. In 1929, the **Yellow Truck & Coach Company** purchased the company, and in 1933, **Chrysler** bought the former Wills factory.

C. Harold Wills moved on to the fledgling **Chrysler Corporation**, where he was awarded many patents on all-steel construction techniques for cars. These techniques included a new form of steel and aluminum alloy that allowed for more flexibility. He also invented a sealed-beam headlight.

Wills died in 1940, still a wealthy man. Marysville never quite lived up to the "Dream City" sobriquet, but the city still opened a museum in honor of C. Harold Wills and the Wills Ste. Claire in 2002.

Not far from Marysville, brothers Fred and Ernest Havers were making their own auto history in 1911. They organized the **Havers Motor Car Company** in Port Huron. Fred was the president, and Ernest designed the six-cylinder, self-starting car produced by the company. The car was advertised with the Havers Self Starting "Six-44" engine as its main selling point. The roadster sold for $1,850, said to be "moderately priced." In 1912, the design changed to that of a touring car. Havers manufactured both two-door and four-door models.

In 1912, the Havers acquired the factory in Port Huron that had previously been used by the **E-M-F** Auto Company. With four years of models from 1911 to 1914, things were going well until July 8, 1914, when a fire destroyed the factory. Although the Havers brothers at first announced intentions to resume production as soon as possible, it ultimately was the end of the Havers automobile of Port Huron, Michigan.

Max and Morris Grabowsky had built a one-ton pickup truck in 1900 and formed the **Rapid Motor Vehicle Company** in Pontiac, Michigan, to market their new truck.

The Havers auto from the Havers brothers in Port Huron was built by the **Havers Motor Car Company** from 1908 until 1914. The auto was discontinued when the **Havers** factory burned down. *Photo by the author.*

The **Rapid Motor Vehicle Company** factory was where trucks and various service vehicles were produced before it was purchased by **GM** and became that company's truck division. *Author's collection.*

In 1895, the **Pontiac Buggy Company** was formed and morphed into the **Pontiac Spring and Wagon Works**. Albert North and Harry Hamilton built the first Pontiac automobile in 1905 and took over the **Rapid Motor Vehicle Company** in the same year. They managed the new company as a separate unit and built lots of different commercial passenger cars, including the Rapid Sight Seeing Car and the Rapid Hotel Bus. All these vehicles seated twelve passengers plus the driver. **Rapid** also began producing one-ton trucks. In 1909, **GM** purchased the **Rapid Motor Vehicle Company**, which transitioned into the **GMC** truck division.

The **Regal Motor Company** started in 1907 and was, at first, located at the corner of Beaubien and Trumbull Streets in Detroit. It sold enough models to move into a new facility in 1908 at 201 Piquette Street at the cross street of Woodward Avenue. The Regal was a five-passenger auto with a four-cylinder, water-cooled engine and a sliding gear and shaft drive. It sold for $1,250. By 1913, the **Regal Motor Company** was producing more than one thousand cars a year. It was also exporting cars to England. The foot pedal throttle and Atwater ignition system contributed to the popularity of the Regal.

In 1915, a V-8 engine was offered, but sales were foundering. By 1917, World War I had created a materials shortage that forced the company to go into receivership. In 1918, the company was sold and the factory was dismantled.

From Bikes to Autos in Jackson, Michigan

The **Jackson Automobile Company** was one of the longer-lived Brass Era automobile companies, named for its birthplace of Jackson, Michigan. The main founder, Byron Carter, started the Steam Job Printing and Rubber Stamp Manufacturing business at 167 Main Street in Jackson in 1885. He was later a proprietor, along with his father, Squire, of a Jackson bicycle shop at the corner of Jackson and Courtland Streets in 1894. Byron Carter built an experimental gasoline auto in 1899 and then used his experience from the steam press to build a steam automobile in 1901. The steam auto design he used was incorporated into the Michigan Steam, a car manufactured in 1902 by the **Michigan Automobile Company** of 45 Monroe Street in Grand Rapids. In 1902, this company also manufactured the Clipper, developed by Elmer Pratt and based on the same steam auto design.

In 1902, Carter formed a partnership with George A. Matthews and Charles Lewis and incorporated the **Jackson Automobile Company**. Both Mathews and Lewis were bank directors. Mathews owned the **Fuller Buggy Company**, which manufactured the Fuller automobile. The **Fuller Buggy Company** was absorbed by the **Jackson Automobile Company**, which had plans to produce both a gasoline auto and a steam-powered auto. They manufactured a car called the Jackson from 1903 until 1923, a steam car called the Jaxon in 1903 and the Orlo in 1904. The Orlo was trumpeted as a car easy to get in and out of because of the door placement. This innovation was added to the 1905 Jackson, and the Orlo was discontinued.

In 1903, the first Jackson auto was a single-cylinder, and the second version in 1904 was a two-cylinder. From 1906 to 1916, the Jackson evolved from a four-cylinder engine to a V-8 engine. One of its slogans was "No hill too steep, no sand too deep."

The 1903 Jaxon was the further development of Carter's steam car, which had three cylinders and six horsepower. Advertisements boasted, "Steam is reliable and easily understood." However, this was the only year that the car was manufactured. A prototype that never quite made it to mass production was the Duck, a car that had the driver in the back seat. This 1913 "back seat driver" model was also called the Jackson Back Seat Steer.

Byron Carter had developed a fixed transmission system that the other two partners didn't want to use in their cars. This disagreement led Carter to quit in 1905. He went on to make the Cartercar. In 1910, Matthews bought out the other partner, Charles Lewis, and installed family members as officers.

Jackson Automobile Factory,
Jackson, Mich.

The **Jackson Automobile Company** started with a one-cylinder car and progressively moved up to building an eight-cylinder. *Author's collection.*

The 1912 Cartercar originally sold for $2,100 and had a friction drive transmission. Cartercars were among the first to feature front doors for the car. *Author's collection.*

Production continued until World War I, when the factory was used for war production. Following the war, the 1921 Princess Coupe came out, but tight credit stifled production. The **Jackson Motor Company** then merged with the **Kentucky Wagon Manufacturing Company** and the **National Motor Company** to form the **Associated Motor Industries**. The 1928 model was the last to use the Jackson nameplate.

Carter moved to Detroit and formed the Cartercar Motor Company, building Cartercars first in Detroit in 1906 and then in 1907 relocating manufacturing to a Pontiac factory. After Carter died from gangrene at the age of forty-four in 1908, **General Motors** purchased the company. Carter had been trying to start his stalled car when the crank kicked back and hit him in the jaw, an injury that resulted in gangrene. This prompted Henry Leland of the **Cadillac Automobile Company** to hasten the invention of the self-starting gasoline engine. Cartercars were discontinued in 1915, and the factory was then used to manufacture the Oakland automobile.

The **Oakland Motor Car Company** was organized in 1907 as the successor to the **Pontiac Buggy Company**. Alanson P. Brush, who had designed the original Cadillac, partnered with Edward Murphy to form the **Oakland Motor Car Company**. For the company's two-cylinder auto, it first used a rotating engine but replaced it with a four-cylinder, forty-horsepower engine the next year. Each succeeding year brought more improvements to the car named the Oakland. By 1910, the company had been purchased by Billy Durant for **GM**, which continued making the Oakland as a division of **GM** until 1932.

Pontiac, named for the Native American chief and the city of Pontiac where it was made, was at first a model that was a marque of the **Oakland Motor Car Company**. However, the name Pontiac proved more popular than its parent marque, and in 1932, the company was renamed the **Pontiac Motor Company**, one of the only known instances where the parent name was replaced by its own brand.

Alanson Brush was a co-founder of the **Oakland Motor Car Company** and was also the owner of the **Brush Runabout Company**, which produced the Brush Runabout in Detroit's Milwaukee Junction. It was a one-cylinder, two-seater car. A bargain at $500, it sold well, and by 1910, ten thousand cars per year were being made. In 1910, the **Brush Runabout Company** became a division of the conglomerate **United States Motor Company** and manufactured cars until it went bankrupt in 1912.

When the **Oakland Motor Car Company** was sold to **GM**, the factory at Oakland Road and Grove Street in Pontiac was purchased by Randall

The 1912 Brush Runabout was produced two years after the company was purchased by the **United States Motor Company**. *Author's collection.*

A. Palmer. He had worked there when it was used to build the Cartercar and knew it was a very good facility. Palmer used the factory to make the Olympian, a motorcar made from 1917 to 1920. Forming the **Olympian Motors Company**, he steadily manufactured low but consistent numbers of the vehicle for three years. In 1920, the company began to hemorrhage money and was taken over by Otis Friend to produce his Friend vehicle in the same factory.

The city of Jackson, Michigan, had other forays into the auto production world besides the **Jackson Motor Company**. The Argo was an auto manufactured by the **Argo Motor Company** of Jackson. The factory used to build the Argo had previously been used by the **Standard Electric Car Company** to build electric cars. The Argo was produced from 1914 to 1918 and then sold to Mansell Hackett, who moved the operation to Grand Rapids and changed the name of the car to the Hackett.

The **Hackett Motor Car Company** built the Hackett from 1916 to 1919. The Hackett was a four-cylinder, 22.5-horsepower car similar to the **Ford** Model T and was available as a four-passenger roadster and a five-passenger touring car. The factory was moved to Grand Rapids in 1918 because of parts shortages caused by World War I. A 1919 model was produced, but it was the last. Chief engineer Fred Guy took his rotary valve engine to Ypsilanti, Michigan, where he built a car called the Ace. The **Hackett Motor Car Company** sold out to the **Lorraine Motors Corporation** in 1919.

The **Lorraine Motors Corporation** used the factory it acquired from **Hackett Motor Car Company** to make its vehicle, the Lorraine. The roadster, coupe, touring and sedan styles were used in models from 1920 to 1922. One of the partners was David Buick, formerly of the **Buick Motor Company**. Trying to build too many models too fast took its toll on the company. The **Lorraine Motors Corporation** filed for bankruptcy in 1922.

Another car company that started in Jackson and moved to Grand Rapids was the **Gem Motor Car Company**. The Gem was a light, four-cylinder touring car, and the Gem Four was a light delivery truck manufactured from 1917 to 1919.

The Briscoe was an auto designed by Benjamin Briscoe and manufactured in Jackson by the **Briscoe Motor Company**, which later became part of the **United States Motor Company**. Benjamin Briscoe was a Detroit engineer and businessman whose first business was manufacturing sheet metal and cans. After helping to finance David Buick's first car, Briscoe decided to produce autos himself.

The **Briscoe Motor Company** was turning out about five cars per day in May 1916. The Briscoe had a four-cylinder, thirty-three-horsepower engine. Its most distinguishing feature was just one headlight in the middle of the radiator grille. Having only one headlight was, unfortunately, illegal in some states. The **Briscoe Motor Company** had four- and eight-cylinder engine models available. You could get the four, and if you decided that you would rather have the eight, they would let you bring the car back, have the eight-cylinder engine installed and only be billed the difference, along with a small installation charge. In 1921, Benjamin Briscoe grew tired of the auto business and sold his company to Clarence A. Earl.

Clarence Earl, upon buying **Briscoe Motor Company**, changed the name to **Earl Motors Inc.** and continued to produce the same car as the Briscoe, only now called the Earl. Still manufactured in Jackson, the first Earl came out in 1921 and had both open and closed models with four-cylinder engines.

The new **Earl Motors Inc.** was, at first, plagued by pranksters when ten thousand unordered menu cards and an expensive set of new awnings for the factory were delivered. Soon, there was more turmoil as Clarence Earl disagreed with his board of directors about the direction of the company.

The Briscoe Touring Car was manufactured by the **Briscoe Motor Company**, one of the businesses of Benjamin Briscoe, who was also instrumental in the histories of the **Maxwell Motor Company** and **Buick Motor Company**. *Author's collection.*

He wanted large volume production, while the board wanted to gradually increase production. Clarence Earl quit in 1922, and the company continued until 1924, having produced about 1,900 vehicles.

The CVI was a car from Jackson manufactured by the **CVI Motor Car Company**, which was in business from 1907 to 1908. The CVI was available as a roadster and touring car with a four-cylinder engine and was mechanically well received but had trouble gaining the financial backing for a second year. The original financers decided they didn't want to be in the car business anymore, so the CVI was only produced as a 1908 model.

The **Clarke-Carter Automobile Company** produced an auto called the Cutting in the Jackson factory where the CVI had been built. The Cutting auto was available in touring and roadster models and was built from 1909 to 1912. The company changed its name to the **Cutting Automobile Company** in 1911. The thirty- to forty-horsepower engine enabled the Cutting to be so fast that Cutting race cars were entered and did well in the Indianapolis 500. In 1912, the Cutting was discontinued due to a shortage of capital.

Another automobile built in Jackson (with a second factory in Chelsea, Michigan) was the Hollier, also known as the Vincent-Hollier. It was the brainchild of Charles Lewis, president of the **Lewis Spring and Axle Company**. The car was produced in the factories of the **Lewis Spring and Axle Company** from 1915 to 1921. The company didn't change its name to **Hollier Motor Company** until 1921. If the name change was to demonstrate how serious the company was about making cars, it came too late, since poor sales of the eight-cylinder, forty-horsepower car caused the company's failure in 1921.

There were at least two different companies called the **Marion Automobile Company**. The first and most notable was in Marion, Ohio, which built an auto called the Marion in 1901. Fred Titus was the owner. This company was very ambitious and released a catalog outlining two different models of steam-powered cars, two different electric cars and a gasoline-powered car it would be producing. However, no other cars were produced besides the 1901 prototypes, although the business remained open as a car repair and parts center. The business was sold to H.T. Love in 1907. Another company called **Marion Motors** made the Marion Flyer in Indianapolis in 1910 and then merged with the **Imperial Motor Company**.

The **Imperial Motor Company** started in Jackson in 1909 and was founded by brothers T.A. and George Campbell. The brothers first owned the **Jackson Carriage Company**. They formed the **Imperial Motor Company** to make a car called the Imperial, which was a mid-size car with a four-cylinder engine. It produced both touring and roadster models from 1909 until 1916. In the spring of 1912, the factory burned down, but the company purchased the old **Buick** truck plant in Jackson and resumed production. **Imperial** merged with **Marion Motors** of Indianapolis to form **Mutual Motors Company**.

Mutual Motors Company produced the Marion-Handley, a car built in Jackson from 1916 to 1917 and the successor to the Marion Flyer. A four-seat roadster and a touring car were offered with six-cylinder engines. The touring car had optional wire wheels to replace the standard wooden artillery wheels. In 1917, it was reported in auto trade magazines that **Mutual Motors Company** would be reorganizing. However, in February 1918, the factory was sold at public auction.

6

SMALL COMPANIES HIT THE MAJORS
FOR A QUICK CUP OF COFFEE

In baseball, when a player is called up from the minors to the majors for just a brief period—for instance, to bat or pitch a few innings—and then sent down to the minors again, it is referred to as "hitting the majors for a quick cup of coffee." The inference is, of course, that they had just enough time to drink a cup of coffee before they were sent back down to the minor leagues. There is even a "Cup of Coffee" club for the players who only played in the majors for a very brief time. In most cases, they played for one game only.

This phrase could also be used to describe a number of companies that had a brief fling at producing an automobile but, for whatever reasons, never got much beyond the planning stage or building a prototype. There were many cup-of-coffee auto companies in Detroit and throughout the Midwest in the early 1900s as cars became a viable alternative to the horse and buggy.

Of the auto companies that hit the majors for a quick cup of coffee, there were more than fifty car models and car companies named "**Eagle**." Many companies appeared less than serious when considering their name choices, which included companies and cars named **Dragon**, **Marvel**, **La Petite**, the **Postal** and the **Little Four**.

The **Aerocar Company** was started by Alexander Y. Malcomson, an immigrant from Scotland who built up a coal business in Detroit in the 1890s, operating six coal yards with thousands of customers. He bought a Winton and realized the potential in the motorcar. In 1905, Malcomson formed the **Aerocar Company** in Detroit and produced two luxury cars, both with four-cylinder engines. One was air-cooled and one water-cooled. Besides a great slogan—"A practical car built by practical people"—and winning a few races, the company couldn't make a go of it and was out of business by 1908. Malcomson was out $90,000 but still had his coal business and plenty of money. The **Aerocar** factory was later used to build the first Hudson auto.

The **Apex Motor Corporation** produced a car called the Ace in Ypsilanti, Michigan, in 1920. F.E. Earnest of Seattle, Washington, traveled to Michigan to see if he could find any cars to sell because there was a shortage after World War I. Not finding the cars he needed, Earnest decided to produce his own and partnered with O.W. Heinz. Together they broke ground in 1919 to build an Ypsilanti auto factory. Three months after the factory was built on South River Street, the first load of Ace cars was on its way to the West Coast.

H.T. Hanover took over the **Apex Motor Corporation** in 1920 and released models named Combat, Scout and Pup because of his penchant for World War I terminology. By 1922, part of the factory was being used by the **Saxon Motor Company**, and by 1923, the entire factory was sold to the **Commerce Motor Truck Corporation**. **H.T. Hanover** moved to Detroit to help promote a taxi called the Diamond. Incidentally, over the years, there were six different cars by six different companies named the Diamond.

The **Barley Motor Car Company** manufactured a car with a six-cylinder, fifty-horsepower Continental engine called the Barley in 1923. The Kalamazoo-produced car didn't have time to add cream or sugar as its cup of coffee ended in 1924.

In 1880, J.P. La Vigne won a gold medal from the Paris Academy of Inventions for an auto line shaft and for the positioning of the engine under the car hood. La Vigne moved to New Haven, Connecticut, from France to continue building automobiles in 1898. In 1901, he moved to Detroit and started **La Vigne Manufacturing Company** to build a three-wheel auto with a three-cylinder engine. He changed the name of the company to **Detroit Automobile Company** and built a four-wheel car called La Petite. By 1905, he had sold more than two hundred of the vehicle. However, in 1906, La Vigne abruptly quit and the company was reorganized. The car was renamed the Paragon and was highly praised, but stiff competition forced the company to go out of business and sell its factory to the **Marvel Motor Company**.

The **Marvel Motor Company** built a two-passenger roadster with a two-cylinder, twelve-horsepower engine at the former factory of the

Detroit Automobile Company in 1906. The factory was at Rivard and Mullet Streets in Detroit. The roadster had rear hub brakes operated by a pedal. The vehicle sold for $800, and the plan was for the factory to produce 325 cars in 1907. The company failed to sell enough autos to turn a profit and declared bankruptcy in early 1907, selling its factory to the **Crescent Motor Car Company**.

The **Crescent Motor Car Company** was poised to keep producing the Marvel runabout auto at a factory it acquired at Monroe and Champlain Streets in Detroit. However, no cars were ever built because the **Crescent Motor Car Company** spent all its capital on buying prototypes. It went out of business in 1909.

The **Dragon Automobile Company** didn't start in Middle Earth or Asgard but in Kittery, Maine, in 1906. When Frank Corlew gained control of the company, he announced a move to Detroit to build the Dragon automobile. Auto trade magazines publicized that **Dragon Automobile Company** had moved to Detroit, but the location was a mystery and led to much press speculation. Finally, it was revealed that it had opened offices in the Campau Building. The first six cars were quickly constructed in a Detroit machine shop in order to present them at the New York Auto Show. The cars were four-cylinder models, with a sliding gear transmission, and highly praised for their craftsmanship and design.

More mystery ensued with **Dragon Automobile Company** when it allegedly got a $136,000 bank loan, using as collateral two hundred Dragon autos completed and locked away in a Philadelphia vault "to be removed therefrom only under the bank's direction and with a percentage of their sale price to be applied as partial payment for the loan," as it read in the loan papers.

In 1907, it was announced that production would be moved from Detroit to a Philadelphia factory formerly used by the **Brill Car Company**. Once located there, the company was served with two legal attachments to its property. The first was by a New Jersey car dealer who complained that three Dragon vehicles delivered to him were defective and repeated requests to repair or recall them had been ignored. The other complaint was from a former employee who said the company owed him $1,700 for back payments and commissions. After that, the engine company that made the Dragon engines sued for non-payment of its bill, and the **Dragon Automobile Company**'s previous landlord sued them for back rent.

The **Dragon Automobile Company** and the company president, John Kane Mills, declared bankruptcy. In April 1908, the **Dragon Automobile**

There were lots of **Dragon Automobile Company** ads, and documents carried the distinctive logo. *Photo by the author, courtesy of the Detroit Automotive Collection.*

Company assets were sold at public auction. However, only six completed autos were ever seen, and the two hundred so-called completed Dragons in the Philadelphia warehouse never materialized.

In later years, the "Little Four" is what the independent auto companies would be called. The Little Four usually included **Hudson**, **Packard**, **Studebaker** and **Nash**. But in 1904, the sobriquet Little Four referred to a steam car exhibited at the Detroit Automobile Show by the **Little Four Automobile Manufacturing Company**. The car was a runabout style that had a three-cylinder steam engine with six to eight horsepower. Limited production caused the company to fail by the end of the year.

Another cup-of-coffee company was created when Fred Postal had a great idea—use his last name as a gimmick to produce a motorcar for postal workers. The **Anderson Machine Company** had just gone out of business in Redford, Indiana, leaving its factory available. The **Postal Automobile**

and Engineering Company was organized in 1906 to produce an auto called the Postal. It was to be a "highwheeler" vehicle, similar to a buggy, with large wagon wheels. Steering was done with a tiller, and it was powered by a two-cylinder, air-cooled engine. Supposedly designed for postal workers, the only difference from its predecessors was fenders on the back wheels. The vehicle that Fred Postal developed was very cumbersome and unsophisticated and very few sold—not even to postal workers.

Kalamazoo, Michigan, had the **Checker Motors Corporation** and also had a number of cup-of-coffee companies. One of the short-lived Kalamazoo car brands was the Michigan, which was produced by the **Michigan Buggy Company** in 1904 by motorizing one of their standard buggies and selling it for $450. The engine was a one-cylinder, three-and-a-half-horsepower engine, and the vehicle had a two-speed transmission with no reverse. The company offered the motorized buggy for a number of years as either the Michigan or, sometimes, the Kalamazoo.

In 1911, the buggy company got more serious about manufacturing autos and formed the **Michigan Motor Car Company**. The car was poised to be a winner, with leather upholstery and a twenty-two-coat paint auto finish. Unfortunately, two of the partners were indicted by a grand jury for a payroll scandal that would have resulted in $100,000 going to the two guilty partners. Called the "Velvet Payroll Scandal" by the press, it was followed by the revelation that another official had lost substantial company money at the racetrack. Still another official was sentenced to two years in jail for mail fraud regarding stock sales. Reorganization of the company by Hugh Chalmers failed, and the plant was sold in 1915 to the **States Motor Car Company**, sometimes known as the **Greyhound Cyclecar Company**. The company used the plant to build its Greyhound car, a four-cylinder, thirty-horsepower roadster. That company had failed by 1918.

The **Handley-Knight Company** built the Handley-Knight in Kalamazoo in 1920 and 1921. It was originally a four-cylinder auto with a Knight "sleeve-valve" engine, but the company switched to a six-cylinder engine in 1922. The cars had small handle attachments that encircled the headlamps; the motto was "If it carries handles, it's a Handley." Founder J.J. Handley announced in 1923 that the company would be building its own engines and would reorganize as **Handley Motors, Inc.** Apparently, it didn't work out because the next year the **Checker Cab Corporation** bought the Handley factory. J.J. Handley announced that an arrangement would probably be worked out to also manufacture the Handley, but that never happened. J.J. Handley's death soon thereafter was listed as a suicide.

The **Roamer Motor Company** started in Streator, Illinois, before moving to Kalamazoo and producing the Roamer, a twenty-three-horsepower vehicle available with a Continental six-cylinder or a Lycoming eight-cylinder engine. It was available in touring, sedan and town car models. Silent film stars Mary Pickford and Buster Keaton owned Roamers, but not too many others did, as the brand went down in flames in 1929, around the time of the stock market crash.

Charles L. Walker was head of the **Walker Motor Car Company**, which manufactured a two-cylinder, ten-horsepower runabout that could seat two passengers. The factory was at 107 Fort Street in Detroit. A 1905 advertisement said, "The runabout is the candy, absolutely noiseless." The ads also said that the "artistic" body made for a "strikingly handsome car." But the car had a poor mechanical history. The factory was closed by authorities in 1906 and the machinery taken to satisfy two judgments totaling $35,000.

The Welch brothers, Allie and Fred, used their bicycle shop in Chelsea, Michigan, to experiment with building auto engines. They built a car to test their engine and were happy enough with it to form the **Welch Motor Company** and show their car, the Welch Tourist, at the Chicago auto show in 1903. When they attempted to manufacture more Welches in Chelsea, they ran into financial difficulties. Regrouping, they moved to Pontiac and started manufacturing again.

The Welch autos were luxurious, and their price reflected it. For $9,000 in 1909 money, one could get a vehicle that had an ice box and sleeping, cooking and dining accommodations for five. Not to mention, it had storage for provisions, hot and cold water in the lavatory and room to comfortably seat nine.

In 1909, Billy Durant purchased the **Welch Motor Company** and added it to the **GM** lineup. **GM** briefly marketed the Welch-Detroit and then retired the brand upon deciding to make Cadillac the luxury car of the **GM** lineup.

7

INDEPENDENT AUTO COMPANIES CONSOLIDATE

Throughout the history of independent auto companies, many of them consolidated with other companies or were taken over by larger companies. **Buick**, **Cadillac**, **Pontiac** and **Chevrolet** were originally independent companies absorbed by **GM**, while **Lincoln Motor Company** became part of **Ford**. **Dodge Jeep**, **Hudson** and **Nash** were separate companies purchased by **Chrysler**.

THE SAD TALE OF DAVID BUICK

David Dunbar Buick (1854–1929) might be the unluckiest auto magnate of all. He was born in Scotland and immigrated with his parents to the United States when he was two. He was coincidentally a foreman in the late 1870s at the James Flower & Brothers Machine Shop at the same time as Henry Ford, although there are no other records of contact between the two auto pioneers.

David Buick went from the James Flower & Brothers Machine Shop to inventing a method for affixing porcelain enamel to cast-iron bathtubs, creating the familiar white bathtub. He soon had thirteen patents, including one for a lawn sprinkler. With his son, Tom, he developed an L-head engine and built an automobile using it in 1900. The auto was built in a barn behind his house on Meldrum Street in Detroit. Buick refined the engine

David Buick first made a fortune by inventing the porcelain enamel still used for the traditional white bathtub. He then designed the first Buick auto. *Author's collection.*

The Buick factory in Flint covered more than three hundred acres and contained more than seven million square feet. *Author's collection.*

with Eugene C. Richard from the **Olds Motor Works**. They perfected a valve in-head engine that had a 20 percent gain over other similar engines.

David Buick was having problems and contacted brothers Frank and Benjamin Briscoe for financing. A car was finished in 1903, but more capital was still needed for further refinements, so Buick went back to the Briscoes for another loan. The Briscoes provided more money and, in the subsequent reorganization, ended up owning 97 percent of the company.

The **Buick Motor Company** incorporated in 1904, but David and Tom Buick only owned a small portion of the stock, which by 1908, they traded in lieu of paying off money owed to the Briscoes. The Briscoes were not very interested in the **Buick Motor Company** once they met future **Maxwell Motor Company** founder Jonathan Maxwell. Because David Buick kept procrastinating on readying the Buick for production, after a year, the Briscoe brothers still had only a prototype auto and a non-producing factory to show for it.

The Briscoes ended up hitching their wagon to Jonathan Maxwell's star as he developed the successful Maxwell automobile. The Buicks sold their interest in **Buick Motor Company** to five investors from the **Flint Wagon**

The **Maxwell Motor Company** was a forerunner of **Chrysler Corporation**. *Author's collection.*

Works. When Billy Durant picked up control, he had a few successful years with the Buick due to its engine. He then used **Buick Motor Company** as a foundation company when he established **GM** in 1908.

David D. Buick was out of the **Buick Motor Company** by 1908 and moved to California, where he organized an oil company. Because of lawsuits over the ownership of the California company's land, the company failed, and Buick was back in Michigan two years later. He then started a carburetor company that also failed.

David Buick tried to form two more auto companies, the **Lorraine Motors Corporation** and the **David Dunbar Buick Company**, which built a car called the Dunbar, but both companies failed. Buick went to Florida during its land boom to become a partner in a real estate firm. When the firm failed, he returned to Detroit, where he was first an instructor and then demoted to working at the information desk of the Detroit School of Trades in 1927. He died in Harper Hospital in 1929, penniless, at the age of seventy-four.

An early work partner of David Buick was Walter Marr of Lexington, Michigan, who stayed with **Buick Motor Company** as chief engineer from 1904 to 1918. He headed his own auto company, the **Marr Auto Car Company**, from 1903 to 1904 to build the Marr Auto Car, a one-cylinder, two-seat runabout with the first tilt steering wheel. When the Elgin, Illinois plant burned to the ground in 1904, Marr teamed with David Buick of Flint to design more improved autos.

MAXWELL MOTOR COMPANY SURVIVES ABSORPTION BY TWO FAILED CONGLOMERATES TO BECOME CHRYSLER

The **Maxwell Motor Company** started as the **Maxwell-Briscoe Motor Company** in Tarrytown, New York, in 1904. Benjamin Briscoe started a sheet-metal stamping business in Detroit at the age of eighteen, which he later sold to the **American Canning Company**. In 1901, Briscoe helped finance David Buick's new motorcar company and, with his brother Frank, became 97 percent owner of the **Buick Motor Company**. When Briscoe met Jonathan D. Maxwell, who had experience at both **Northern Manufacuting Company** and **Olds Motor Works**, he sold his interest in Buick (after attempting a consolidation of the two companies) and formed a new partnership to manufacture the Maxwell—a two-cylinder, water-cooled car—in 1905. The models first offered were a two-passenger tourabout for $750 and a five-passenger touring car for $1,400. These cars were well received by the public, and by 1907, following a fire at the Tarrytown, New York site, branch factories were established in Auburn, New York; Pawtucket and Cranston, Rhode Island; and a large one in New Castle, Indiana, an Indianapolis suburb.

The Maxwell enjoyed high production and sales throughout the early 1900s. In 1910, production exceeded twenty thousand autos. Sales were helped by the promotional stunts orchestrated by sales manager Cadwallader Washburn Kelsey. Kelsey had the Maxwell climbing up the steps of famous buildings (even churches), balanced on teeterboards and even staged police chases. These antics would be captured on film and viewed in the early nickelodeons of the day. The Maxwell also achieved acclaim in car races and cross-country treks.

In 1910, the **Maxwell Motor Company** was purchased by William Durant to be part of his conglomerate, the ill-fated **United States Motor Company**, of which the Maxwell auto was the only profitable component.

As auto companies faced stiff competition from one another, many combined forces. This increased profitability by combining factories and labor forces, or to offer more model choices, increase the sales network

The 1907 Maxwell-Briscoe Roadster was manufactured before the company joined the U.S. Motor Company. *Author's collection.*

or other combinations of factors. Probably the most well-known auto conglomeration is **GM**. The original car companies and nameplates that combined or were purchased to form **GM** include **Buick**, **Olds**, **Cadillac** and **Oakland**, which became **Pontiac**. **GM** also purchased the companies that made the Cartercar, Elmore, Ewing, Rapid and Chevrolet.

Durant Motors was incorporated in 1923 by Billy Durant after he was with **GM**. **Durant Motors** had an auto lineup that included cars named the Flint, Durant and Star that were meant to compete with **General Motors**. **Mason Truck Company** was part of the **Durant Motors** lineup. The last model **Durant Motors** manufactured was the Durant, which was produced in a Lansing factory in 1931.

A not-as-well-known auto conglomeration was the **United States Motor Company**. In 1908, Benjamin Briscoe of **Briscoe Motor Company** and **Buick Motor Company** attempted to consolidate **Maxwell-Briscoe** and **Buick Motor Company** into a single company under the name **International Motor Company** but to no avail. In 1909, the company name was changed to **United States Motor Company**, or **USMC** for short. By 1910, the **USMC** began picking up automotive companies that had been experiencing trouble getting financing on their own. These companies included **Stoddard-Dayton**, the **Courier Car Company**, the **Columbia Automobile Company**, **Maxwell Motor Company**, **E.R. Thomas-Detroit Company**, **Alden Sampson Trucks**, **Gray Marine** and **Providence Engineering Works**.

After a successful 1910, using its eighteen plants with a combined floor space of forty-nine acres, **USMC** produced fifteen thousand Maxwells, ten thousand Brush Runabouts and ten thousand of the Stoddard-Dayton, Columbia and Alden Sampson Trucks. In 1911, **USMC** offered fifty-two models. However, in September 1912, the company went into receivership. The owners claimed that it was due to the bankers not extending enough credit, and the bankers blamed the company directors for poor management.

The assets of the **USMC** and its constituent companies were sold at a public foreclosure auction for $7,080,000 in January 1913. It was purchased by Jonathan Maxwell and Walter Flanders, formerly of the **E-M-F Company** and **Flanders Electric Auto Company**, respectively. They went on to reorganize as the **Maxwell Motor Company** in 1914. The Maxwell was the only auto from the **USMC** group to continue to be manufactured. Because the Tarrytown, New York factory had been sold to **GM** to manufacture its new Chevrolet, **Maxwell Motor Company** relocated to Detroit. Truck and bus production that had started in 1905 continued at the new Detroit location. The Maxwell came out as a six-cylinder, although the four-cylinder models were offered up until the last Maxwell came out in 1925. **Maxwell Motor Company** had a very popular vehicle for physicians called the Dr. Maxwell.

In 1920, Maxwell dealers suffered a crunch when there were more than seventeen thousand overstocked Maxwells, due to the post–World War I recession. The company tried uniting with **Chalmers Motor Car Company** in 1922 but still struggled. The next year, Walter Chrysler joined the company and proceeded to repair much of the damage of previous years. This effort included a public relations move to repair for free many of the defective Maxwells that had recently been released. In 1924, Walter Chrysler became president of the **Chalmers-Maxwell Motor Company**, which released a car called the Chrysler and the last Maxwell. By mid-1925, the company name was changed to the **Chrysler Corporation**. The Maxwell is best remembered in pop culture as the car that Jack Benny rode in when appearing on his popular comedy radio and television shows.

In 1922, the **Associated Motor Industries** was formed in Dayton, Ohio, of various auto companies. These companies included the **Jackson Motor Corporation** of Jackson, Michigan; the **National Motor Car and Vehicle Corporation** of Indianapolis; and the **Kentucky Wagon Manufacturing Company** of Louisville, which was the company that manufactured the Dixie Flyer.

ROY CHAPIN AND FRIENDS GUIDE HUDSON TO THIRD PLACE

The **Hudson Motor Car Company** was one of the major auto companies of its day, ranking in the top seven for auto sales in the years it was in existence. **Hudson** was formed by Roy Chapin, who, like Henry Ford, was one of the giants of the early auto industry.

Roy Chapin (1889–1935) was born in Lansing, Michigan, in 1880. A true entrepreneur, he had a successful photography business before he graduated from high school. In 1899, Chapin entered the University of Michigan and joined the near-bankrupt fraternity Phi Delta Theta as business manager. He soon turned the fraternity back toward solvency.

While at the University of Michigan, sales-whiz Chapin met future engineers Howard Coffin and Roscoe Jackson, his future partners in the formation of **Hudson Motor Car Company**. Howard Coffin was a master engineer who built his first gasoline-powered car in 1897 and a steam-powered car in 1898 while he worked on his engineering degree, which he completed in 1902. Roscoe Jackson was a talented businessman and engineer.

Roy Chapin didn't finish college due to a ride in an Oldsmobile on Grand Boulevard in Detroit in 1901. After the ride, he reportedly said, "This is the stuff for me. I'm going to quit school and join up!" Join up he did, as he started working for **Olds Motor Works**. His friends Coffin and Jackson followed him and joined **Olds** after they graduated. Also at **Olds** was future **Hudson** co-

Roy Chapin knew from his first ride in an auto that car manufacturing was what he wanted to do. He is pictured here as secretary of commerce in the Hoover Cabinet. *Courtesy of the Library of Congress.*

founder Frederick O. Bezner and his friend James J. Brady, who is credited with coining the name "Oldsmobile" and saving the Curved Dash Olds prototype from the fire that destroyed the first Olds factory.

The charismatic Roy Chapin was soon made the sales agent for **Olds**. Part of his promotion involved personally driving the Curved Dash Olds from Detroit to New York City.

By 1903, control of the **Olds Motor Works** had passed from founder Ransom E. Olds to copper tycoon Fredric Smith, who had invested $200,000. Olds clashed with Smith over the future of the company; Smith wanted to make luxury cars while Ransom Olds wanted to make cars the average workingman could afford. The future **Hudson** founders, Roy Chapin and friends, weren't happy with the changing product lines, and after two years, they had left the company with the intention of forming their own.

The first venture of the fledgling group was building Howard Coffin's car design for the **E.R. Thomas Motor Company**. With an initial order of five hundred cars, the group had its first office in the Majestic Building in Detroit and rented a twenty-thousand-square-foot building to build its car, dubbed the Thomas Flyer. The name of the company changed to the **E.R. Thomas-Detroit Company**.

Hugh Chalmers bought half of Thomas's stock, and the company name became the **Chalmers-Detroit Motor Company**. With Thomas and Chalmers each owning one-third of the stock and Chapin, Coffin, Brezny and Brady the other third, the company came out with a new Howard Coffin–designed car known as the Chalmers-Detroit 30 in 1908. The new car was a great success, and soon, Roy Chapin and his partners wanted more control over the company.

Hugh Chalmers and the **Chalmers-Detroit Motor Company** continued manufacturing cars. In 1911, the name was changed to just the **Chalmers Motor Car Company**, dropping Detroit from the company name. It produced touring and roadster models as well as acquiring the Brush Runabout rights.

The company flourished in the 1910s with its best year in 1911, when it was the number-eight auto producer in the United States. In 1910, it became known for issuing the Chalmers Award in baseball to the "most important and useful player to the club and to the league." However, when the World War I recession hit the company, it had some bad years financially. In the early 1920s, it merged with the **Maxwell Motor Company**. The last Chalmers nameplate on a vehicle was in 1923.

Wanting more control, Chapin and Coffin, along with Brezny, Jackson and Brady, formed the **Hudson Motor Car Company** on October 28, 1908. Joseph L. Hudson agreed to become a financial partner and the company's largest investor. Hudson owned a department store also named for him, the J.L. Hudson Company. Although the auto company was named for Hudson, he was a silent partner (by choice), and Chapin and associates (Coffin, Brezny, Jackson and Brady) were clearly in charge. Hugh Chalmers and Lee Counselman were also big stockholders.

Many car nameplates were named for the car's designer, including Chevrolet, Buick, Ford and Dodge. The chief designer for the Hudson auto was Howard Coffin, which might have been one of the reasons the company was named for Hudson. The new car company owners must have realized that a car named the "Coffin" or the "Coffinmobile" might have been a hard-sell.

The newly formed **Hudson Motor Car Company** purchased an eighty-thousand-square-foot factory at Mack Avenue and Beaufait Street in Detroit. This was the factory used to build the Aerocar from 1905 to 1908. In 1909, the **Hudson Motor Car Company** built its first car, the Hudson Twenty, which sold for $900 and became an immediate success. In the first year, the company sold 1,100 vehicles and had thousands on order. By the following July, it had sold over 14,000 Hudsons.

Chalmers Motor Car Co., Detroit, Mich.

The **Chalmers Motor Car Company** had a few good years before merging with **Maxwell Motor Company**. *Author's collection.*

The 1912 Hudson was built in the first **Hudson** factory. The **Hudson** founders had been co-owners of the **Chalmers Motor Car Company** before forming the **Hudson Motor Car Company**. *Author's collection.*

The first Hudson factory, on Mack Avenue and Beaufait Street in Detroit, was also used to make the Aerocar. *Photo by Lynn Lyon.*

The Hudson was at first assembled from parts manufactured by other companies, with none of the components manufactured by Hudson. In 1911, Hudson offered **Continental Motors Company** of Muskegon, Michigan, a contract to produce ten thousand engines for it, triggering **Continental Motors** to build a new factory in Detroit on land sold to it by the **Hudson Motor Car Company**. **Continental** later produced its own autos in 1932 and 1933.

By 1913, **Hudson** had a new factory, designed by Albert Kahn, the same architect who built some of Detroit's most noteworthy buildings and auto factories and who was instrumental in using reinforced steel in his factories. The factory was located on Jefferson Avenue at the crossroad of Conner Avenue in Detroit near Grosse Pointe and the one-time village of Fairview. It was used to produce Coffin's new design, a six-cylinder car that could reach sixty-five miles per hour. The following year, all of **Hudson**'s cars had a six-cylinder engine, and **Hudson** billed itself as the "world's largest manufacturer of six-cylinder cars." In 1916, all Hudsons had a "self-starter," replacing the hated crank starter. In fact, when cranking a car didn't work, the car was said to be "cranky," adding a new adjective to the American lexicon.

In January 1916, the Hudson Super Six came out and right away set a new speed record of 102.5 miles per hour. Later that year, the vehicle set a record for climbing Pikes Peak in eighteen minutes and twenty-five seconds. In September 1916, three men drove the Super Six touring car from San Francisco to New York in five days, three hours and thirty-one minutes—a new record. They then completed the first double transcontinental tour by turning around and driving right back to San Francisco. This was wonderful publicity for **Hudson** and resulted in doubling sales in 1916 to more than twenty-five thousand cars, selling more sedans than the **Ford** and **Chevrolet** brands combined.

The Super Six kept Hudson among the top-selling car companies for more than a decade. In 1928, it introduced the ninety-one horsepower Special Six. The company had its best year in 1929, producing more than 300,000 cars. This made **Hudson** the number three automaker behind **Ford** and **GM**.

In 1917, the **Hudson Motor Car Company** leased an old **Studebaker** plant on Franklin Avenue in Detroit to build the Essex, a smaller version of the Super Six. They got the name Essex from looking at a map of England. The Essex soon set records of its own, including completing a transcontinental cruise in only four days, twenty-one hours and thirty-two minutes. Probably even more important sales-wise was that it was a successful closed coach model. In 1922, the Essex was the most inexpensive closed coach sedan in the United States at only $1,495. Essex sales continued for another ten years, until 1933.

A new **Hudson** factory was built at Jefferson and Conner Streets in Detroit in the 1920s.
Courtesy of the Ypsilanti Automotive Heritage Museum.

The Spectacular New Hudson WASP

HOLLYWOOD

You can see the style . . . come try the power!

The Hudson Wasp was built by both the **Hudson** and the **American Motors Company** in the 1950s. **AMC** was formed by a merger between the **Hudson** and **Nash** auto companies. *Author's collection.*

In 1932, the Terraplane was introduced as an Essex model. It was called the Terraplane due to the popularity of anything to do with planes. The first Terraplane was given to aviation pioneer Orville Wright and the second one went to aviatrix Amelia Earhart, both of whom were involved in the promotion of the vehicle. To further its identification with flying machines, the Terraplane was said to make one feel like they were "land flying." In 1933, the Essex name was dropped, and the Terraplane name took precedence. The Terraplane nameplate was successful and was therefore incorporated back into the **Hudson** fold as the Hudson Terraplane in 1938. However, very soon the glory days of the Terraplane were over, and the name was dropped in 1939.

The **Hudson Motor Car Company** made it through the Great Depression and in 1941 posted profits of $3,756,000. In February 1942, the Hudson Company converted to war production, building machine guns and aircraft parts. After the war, **Hudson** sold somewhat updated versions of its 1942 models for its 1946 and 1947 lines.

In 1948, **Hudson** introduced a new "step down" design, which referred to placement of the passenger compartment down inside the perimeter of the frame so that the passenger could step down into the car. Successful to the tune of $13.2 million in 1949, most of the following models were similar until 1951, when the "Fabulous Hudson Hornet" was introduced. With a Super Six–cylinder, 308-inch-square engine, the Hornet was a stock car race champion, coming in first overall in the NASCAR circuit in 1952. Also in 1952, a vehicle with a 262-inch-square engine called the Wasp was developed as a smaller companion car to the Hornet.

In 1952, **Hudson** brought out a compact car, the Hudson Jet. Unfortunately, sales were a disaster due to compact car competition from **Ford**, **Chevrolet** and **Plymouth** that same year. The sporty Hudson Italia, designed in Italy, was too little too late, and **Hudson Motor Car Company** could see the writing on the wall. Poor sales coupled with labor strikes led **Hudson** to enter talks to consolidate with the **Nash-Kelvinator Corporation** in 1954. By 1955, **Hudson** was part of **American Motors Company**, and by 1957, the Hudson nameplate disappeared.

"ASK THE MAN WHO DRIVES ONE"

Packard Motor Company

The **Packard Motor Car Company** started as the **Ohio Automobile Company** of Warren, Ohio, in 1899. James Packard purchased the twelfth Winton horseless carriage from the Winton factory in Cleveland. However, it broke down while he was trying to drive the sixty miles home to Warren. He had to have it towed by a team of plow horses, and once he got it home, he tinkered with it to find out why it broke down. Good mechanic that he was, he found and corrected many problems, and when he again saw Alexander Winton, he gave him some suggestions on his vehicle. Alex Winton was not good at taking criticism and told Packard that if he knew so much, he should start his own company, which Packard did.

Packard hired George Weiss and W.A. Hatcher away from Winton in 1899 and had them design the first Packard, a one-cylinder, seven-horsepower vehicle driven by a chain drive leading to the rear wheels. The Packard was so popular that four more units were assembled and sold right away.

In 1899, James Packard formed the **Ohio Automobile Company** with his brothers, Weiss and Hatcher. A sales agency was opened in New York to sell Packards and try to raise capital for a larger operation. When Henry B. Joy traveled to New York to purchase a vehicle, he witnessed two Packards take off to chase a fire engine. He was impressed by the way the vehicles began instantly. He purchased the only other Packard left in the city and drove it back to his home in Detroit.

Henry B. Joy's father was James Frederick Joy, one of the founders of the Republican Party and instrumental in reviving the Michigan Southern Railroad. The elder Joy was very involved in the push to build a railroad line to Missouri and obtaining funding for the Soo Locks. He hired Abraham Lincoln when Lincoln was beginning his law practice to help with railroad mergers. His son, Henry, was also a successful businessman when he saw and purchased his Packard auto.

Henry Joy secured financing for the Packard brothers from the sons of the Detroit business stalwarts of the 1900s. Among them were seed tycoon Dexter Ferry's son, lumber baron Russell Alger's son, millionaire Senator James McMillan's son Phillip and the son of Charles DuCharme of the Michigan Stove Company. It's interesting that in all these cases, it was the son of the tycoon who put up the money. Henry B. Joy was named president of the company.

By 1903, the Packard brothers were pretty much out of the picture as far as running the company operations. They would later sell their stock and exit the company completely. The **Packard Motor Car**

The Packard Plant was trail-blazing with the world's first use of reinforced concrete. *Author's collection.*

Company built a new auto plant in Detroit in 1903 designed by architect Albert Kahn, and in 1905, Kahn designed the famed Building 10 of the **Packard** complex. Building 10 was the first in the world to be constructed of reinforced concrete. In 1904, the company produced its first trucks, at first to help in the construction of its own plants and after that to sell to the public.

Henry Joy led the company through many prosperous years, and in 1916, he became the chairman of the board. He was instrumental in starting aircraft engine manufacturer **Liberty Motors** and was in on the development of the V-12 engine, used in many aircraft of the day. He would later purchase land in the Mt. Clemens/Chesterfield Township area and build Joy Air Field, one of the first airfields in the nation. This airfield was purchased by the government during World War I and renamed Selfridge Air Base, named for Thomas Selfridge, who in 1908 was the first man to be killed in a plane crash. The street adjoining the base is still known as Joy Road for Henry Joy. It is fitting to have a road named for him since Joy was one of the main sponsors of the Lincoln Highway Association, which was dedicated to building a concrete road from San Francisco to New York. Joy lived to see the road completed.

By savvy marketing and selling a lower-priced automobile, **Packard Motor Car Company** survived the Great Depression and, in 1937, was the ninth largest auto company in the United States. **Packard** continued to sell medium-priced autos and did well in the 1940s. With more than $8 million in cash reserves, the company realized that because of the rising post–World War II prices for tools, dyes and various other components needed for auto production, it would be a good time to acquire a partner auto company to share expenses.

The **Packard Motor Car Company** was heavily courted by **Nash Motors** to join its conglomerate of **Nash** and **Hudson**. With lots of offers to choose from, **Packard** eventually struck up a deal with **Studebaker Corporation** in 1956. The production of new Packards was moved to the **Studebaker** factory in Indiana, and thereafter, the Packard story coincided with that of Studebaker.

A Wisconsin connection to the independent auto company story began with the **Mitchell Motor Company** of Racine, Wisconsin. It was started by William Turner Lewis after he married the daughter of Henry Mitchell, proprietor of the **Mitchell and Lewis Wagon Company**. In the 1890s, the wagon company spun off the **Wisconsin Wheel Works** to manufacture bicycles. In 1901, the **Wisconsin Wheel Works** started

The abandoned 1903 Packard factory on East Grand Boulevard in Detroit has become a symbol of industrial blight. *Photo by the author.*

For a brief time after the **Studebaker-Packard** merger, the **Packard** plant was used for co-production of the company's cars. In 1958, the operations were moved to the **Studebaker** plant in South Bend, Indiana, and operations ceased in Detroit. *Photo by the author.*

The **Mitchell Company** started out making wagons, added bicycle manufacturing and finally became a car manufacturer. *Author's collection.*

producing a motorized bicycle, also called a motorcycle. It wasn't a success because it was so slow a bicycle could overtake it.

The name of the company was changed in 1903 to reflect its new calling—producing motorcars. The new name became the **Mitchell Motor Company**. The bicycle business was sold to an Indiana firm, and although the wagon business stayed around awhile longer, in 1917, it too was sold so that the only focus was producing motorcars.

The company's first motorcars produced for 1904 were chain driven and had two-cylinder engines cooled by water and steered with a tiller. The 1905 model allowed a choice between water- and air-cooled engines. All the cars the company produced had four-cylinder engines by 1907, and by 1910, **Mitchell Motor Company** provided a wide choice of models. The company merged with a farm machine manufacturing company and became the **Mitchell-Lewis Motor Company**.

Cracks in the façade began when William Mitchell Lewis, the son of William Turner Lewis, broke away from the company and formed the **Lewis Motor Company** to produce a car designed by French designer Rene Petard. The company manufactured a touring model in 1914 and both a touring and a roadster model in 1915. However, World War I intruded,

Rene Petard got called back to France and W.M. Lewis disbanded his company. Unusual for the day, Lewis not only paid in full all 280 employees, he also found new jobs in Racine and surrounding communities for them.

Meanwhile, the **Mitchell-Lewis Motor Company** reorganized as the **Mitchell Motor Company** in 1916, and sales manager Otis Friend took over as president—that is, until Otis proved no friend to the company as he left to build his own short-lived vehicle, the Friend, in Pontiac, Michigan. Friend took over the presidency of the **Olympian Motors Company** and produced the Olympian brand until his own car was ready. The renamed **Friend Motor Company** produced three models for the New York Auto Show. It took orders for more units but never produced any because of insufficient financing. Bankruptcy followed, and the factory, which had first produced the Cartercar and then the Olympian, was sold to the highest bidder. The last time anyone saw Otis Friend, he was in Warren, Ohio, trying to finance a company to be called the **Colonial Motor Company**, with plans to produce a car called the Colonial. This time, he didn't find any financial backing.

For 1916, the **Mitchell Motor Company** produced a V-8 engine and made the six-cylinder the standard size, jettisoning the four-cylinder engine once and for all. Sales continued to be good until 1920, when the design department presented a sloping radiator configuration that was dubbed the "Drunken Mitchell." The next year, the "design flaw" was corrected, but sales had peaked. The company hit a bad patch in 1922 and filed for bankruptcy. The last car released was the 1923 model, after which the company was sold to the **Nash Motors Company**.

The **Thomas B. Jeffery Company** started making motorcars in Kenosha, Wisconsin, in 1902. The company had two nameplates, the Rambler and, later, the Jeffery, named for the founder. The company had started as **Gormully and Jeffrey Manufacturing** and originally made bicycles. Thomas Jeffery built his first motorcar in 1897 and convinced the bicycle company to finance his new invention to sell it to the public. It was a success, and the firm began building motorcars.

After Thomas died in 1910, his son, Charles, became president. He introduced two major features to motorcars—a front-mounted engine and the steering wheel. The Jeffery was also the second to use an assembly line—the **Olds Motor Works** was the first.

In 1916, Charles Jeffery sold the company to Charles Nash, who had quit **GM** (even though he had married the boss's daughter), to run the company. In 1917, he renamed it **Nash Motors** for himself. Almost joining him was Walter Chrysler, who would later quit **GM** to form the **Chrysler Corporation**. In 1917, **Nash Motors** produced its last Jeffery. The next year, the car nameplate became the Nash.

Charles Nash Advances from Indentured Servant to Auto Company Tycoon

Nash Motors was started by and named for Charles W. Nash (1864–1948). **Nash** arose from humble beginnings, working as an indentured servant in Genesee County, where Flint is located, from ages seven to twelve. He was abandoned to the state when his parents divorced and given a contract that stated he would work for free on a "sponsor's" farm for room and board. At age twenty-one, he would be awarded $100 and a new suit of clothes from his "sponsor."

Fleeing the restrictive contract forced upon him, he next became a farm worker and entrepreneur, buying and selling sheep and wool. He soon established himself in the business world and was eventually hired by the **Flint Road Cart Company** in 1891, when he was twenty-seven years old. This company became the **Durant-Dort Carriage Company**, and this put **Nash** on the ground floor of early car producers in the United States as **Durant-Dort** went from being a buggy manufacturer to one of the first car producers. **Nash** was eventually the top executive in the firm.

The reason Flint was originally known as the "Vehicle City" was because of the number of buggy makers there. After David Buick developed the **Buick Motor Company** in 1903, interest in the motorcar began to peak in the Flint area. **Durant-Dort** and other Flint companies that were making buggies decided to switch to motorcars. David Buick, upon inventing the engine for his namesake car, allowed the company to be bought by the largest stockholders, Frank and Benjamin Briscoe. They moved the company from its Detroit starting point to Flint.

In August 1910, Charles Nash moved from the **Durant-Dort Carriage Company** to become one of the owners of **Buick** and to supervise production in Flint. The **Buick** line became part of Billy Durant's **GM** in 1908 but was operated as a separate division and nameplate. Nash guided it to profitability and became general manager of **GM**.

In 1916, he bought out the **Thomas B. Jeffery Motor Company** and renamed it **Nash Motors**.

Charles W. Nash overcame humble beginnings to become a trail-blazing leader in the auto industry. *Courtesy of the Library of Congress.*

In 1925, a subsidiary brand of **Nash**, the Ajax Six, was introduced. When the **Mitchell Motor Company** went bankrupt, **Nash** beat the **Hupp Motor Car Company**'s bid for the Mitchell factory by a mere $5,000. The Ajax was built in this factory in Racine, Wisconsin.

The Ajax was offered as a four-door sedan model and a touring model. However, as a result of light sales, the name was changed to the Nash Light Six, and sales improved with the more well-known Nash name. To complete the transformation of an Ajax to a Nash Light Six, **Nash Motors** offered a kit to Nash dealers containing grille badges and hubcaps to exchange for the Ajax equivalents. The 1920s were good years for **Nash Motors**, as the company enjoyed continued profitability under Charles Nash. The 1930s saw a decline in sales, but **Nash Motors** was the only auto company besides **GM** to record a profit in the Great Depression year of 1932.

Charles Nash served as president of the **Lafayette Motor Company** at the same time as he was president of **Nash Motors**. The **Lafayette Motor Company** was originally from Indianapolis and made luxury cars in 1920. In 1921, **Nash** bought the majority interest in **Lafayette Motor Company**. For a while, the two companies operated separately. The

Lafayette auto was named for the Marquis de Lafayette and had a cameo of the marquis for its logo. It was the first car to have an electric clock.

In 1922, **Nash Motors** moved its headquarters to Milwaukee, Wisconsin. In 1924, Charles Nash became full owner of **Lafayette Motor Company** and combined the two companies while retiring the Lafayette name until 1934, when it was reintroduced as a **Nash Motors Company** model, this time a smaller version of the luxury car. In 1937, it was named the Nash Lafayette 400 and was the lowest-priced **Nash** vehicle until 1940, when it was discontinued.

Charles Nash continued to drive **Nash Motors** to profitability until he stepped down in 1937—after engineering the successful merger between appliance manufacturer Kelvinator and **Nash Motors**. He was also responsible for the hiring of his successor, Charles W. Mason. Nash died in 1948 at his Beverly Hills, California home. He was eighty-four.

Nash-Kelvinator thrived during the rest of the 1930s, and when the United States entered World War II in 1941, the company switched to producing war materials like many other car manufacturers. After the war, the economic situation began to get harder for the smaller, independent motor companies.

The Mitchell auto of the **Mitchell Motor Company** is shown in the window of the **Gilson Auto Company**, an auto dealership. *Author's collection.*

With many auto companies going under, it did not seem to be a good time for a new company to start, but **Crosley Motor Company** had the backing of the Crosley Corporation and its boss, industrialist Powel Crosley Jr. The Crosley empire already included a broadcasting company and the Cincinnati Reds baseball team, but Powel Crosley felt that the auto market was lacking a niche in the subcompact market. Emulating fellow industrialist Henry J. Kaiser, Crosley started having his brother, Lewis, help him design some of his automotive ideas.

Using assembly plants in Richmond and Marion, Indiana, the company produced a car called the Crosley. The first model in 1939, a two-seat convertible, was sent back to the drawing board for improvements, such as universal joints, but soon, the company had a variety of models for its 1941 lineup. These included two- and four-passenger convertibles, a station wagon, a convertible sedan and a pickup.

Two notable Crosley models included one called the Parkway Delivery, which was a mini-panel truck with no roof over the front seat, and another one called the Covered Wagon. The Covered Wagon was a pickup truck with a removable top and a removable back seat.

The Crosley proved very popular in the early years of World War II when gas rationing started. Most of the Crosleys could get fifty miles per gallon and fit in well with the government plan to use less gasoline. **Crosley Motor Company** became the last civilian car company to convert to war production in late 1942.

Crosley Motor Company resumed regular auto production in 1946 at the Marion, Indiana facility. It had sold the Richmond factory during the war. Before the war, the Crosley line was air-cooled, and after the war, the whole line was cooled by water. The 1948 vehicle was the first to be termed a "sport utility" vehicle. Crosleys also had the first all-steel wagon bodies in 1947 and were the first American car to be fitted with four-wheel caliper disc brakes.

The **Crosley Motor Company**'s best year was 1948, when sales reached almost 25,000 automobiles. Thereafter, sales and production declined until 1952, when only 1,522 Crosley vehicles were sold. Attempts to stop the decline by building and selling a farm utility vehicle, the Farm-O-Road, and a sports car, the Crosley Hotshot, were unsuccessful.

In 1952, production ceased in July, and the Marion, Indiana plant was sold to the General Tire and Rubber Company. Talks with **Nash Motors Company** to buy **Crosley Motor Company** didn't result in a merger, as **Nash Motors** partnered with the **Hudson Motor Car Company** instead. Many of the **Crosley** models and vehicles, such as the 1950 Crosley Hotshot sports car, are fondly remembered.

The new American car startups after World War II were few and far between. One of the few was the **Tucker Motor Company**, started by Preston Tucker to show what could be done to make a better car. In 1948, the major automakers weren't putting out new models after the war production of the mid-1940s; therefore, new safety features were not being incorporated. Tucker designed his car with all the latest features, including a padded dashboard, a water-cooled aluminum block, disc brakes, four-wheel independent suspension, fuel injection and more.

The premiere of the Tucker 48, named for the founder and the year it came out, was plagued with problems. The car suffered mechanical problems during its first big showing, and at the unfortunate climax of the presentation, the Tucker started emitting plumes of smoke as it went offstage.

Other forces were against the Tucker; the **Tucker Motor Company** was sued by the Big Three companies, and it had to spend lots of money to defend against the deep pockets of the Big Three. This was one of the main reasons the company produced only fifty-one Tuckers.

The **Tucker Motor Company**'s story was told in a highly acclaimed movie by Francis Ford Coppola in 1988, *Tucker: The Man and His Dream.*

A Tucker auto is shown in front of Preston Tucker's Ypsilanti home at 110 North Park Street. Tucker's workshop was in the back. *Courtesy of the Ypsilanti Automotive Heritage Museum.*

Another new postwar car marque that had a movie connection was the DeLorean. It was produced by the **DeLorean Motor Company** and had its greatest fame as the car that broke the time barrier in the movie *Back to the Future*. Its founder and designer was John DeLorean, who gained renown as a designer for **General Motors** when he designed the Pontiac Firebird, Pontiac Grand Prix and Pontiac GTO. The **DeLorean Motor Company** was formed in 1975 and produced one model—the DeLorean DMC-12 with gull-wing doors. Due to production delays, the car wasn't released until 1981.

Founder and designer John DeLorean was arrested for drug trafficking in October 1982 but was acquitted after proving police entrapment. However, the damage had been done, and the **DeLorean Motor Company** declared bankruptcy and called it quits in 1984. The late Johnny Carson owned a DeLorean, as does retired late-night host Jay Leno.

Tesla Motors of Lyndhurst, Ohio, started producing electric cars in 2003. Present models include the Tesla Roadster and a sedan style, the Model S. They are produced in Fremont, California, in the former factory used for the joint venture between **Toyota Motor Corporation** and **GM** in the early 1990s, **New United Motors Manufacturing** (**NUMMI**). **Tesla Motors** has produced over fifty thousand electric cars so far.

8

THE "LITTLE FOUR" BECOME JUST TWO

As the smaller companies began to succumb to the market forces of the 1940s, the number of smaller, independent auto companies had shrunk down to **Nash**, **Hudson**, **Studebaker**, **Packard**, **Willys-Overland**, **Crosley** and **Checker Cab**. **Graham-Paige** had reorganized with Henry J. Kaiser and Joseph Frazer to become **Kaiser-Frazer** in 1948.

In 1954, the two largest auto companies, **GM** and **Ford**, battled each other for supremacy in the "family car" business. **GM**'s Chevrolet marque had been the leader for a long time in sales to the largest market niche—families with children—and **Ford Motor Company** was ready to lower prices to beat them. This price war between the two largest auto companies played havoc with sales for the independents, and **Packard**, **Nash**, **Hudson** and **Studebaker** all had bad years with much lower sales than the previous year. Relative newcomer **Kaiser-Frazer** had the worst year of all.

By early 1954, the remaining independents investigated aligning with one another. After World War II, the costs for tooling and dies had gone sky-high. These increases drove up the costs for developing the new models the public wanted. The independent auto companies realized they could no longer afford to produce new models on their own. However, by teaming up with other companies, they could make new models with variations on shared frames or body shells to reduce overall costs.

Hudson and Nash Merge to Form American Motors Company

The first of the postwar independents to merge were **Kaiser-Frazer** and **Willys-Overland**, who joined forces in 1953. The others—**Studebaker, Hudson, Nash** and **Packard**—were referred to as the "Little Four" in the late 1940s. **Nash** was still profitable due to its Kelvinator appliance division. **Nash**'s president, George M. Mason, first began talks with **Hudson** and **Packard**, and then, **Studebaker** began talks with **Packard**.

Meeting in room 2607 of the Book-Cadillac Hotel in Detroit on June 16, 1953, **Nash** president Mason and **Hudson** president A.E. Barit agreed to combine forces. By early 1954, **Hudson** dealers were selling a slightly different version (grille badge and hubcaps) of the sub-compact Nash Metropolitan, a nicely styled, well-accepted and dependable vehicle. This model was in addition to the Hudson Hornet, Hudson Wasp and the smaller, sales-challenged Hudson Jet.

The new merger of **Nash** and **Hudson** was named **American Motors Company**, or **AMC**, by George Mason and was the biggest alliance in the history of the auto industry up to that point.

Mason, once he had **Hudson** on board, made a pitch to **Packard**'s president, James J. Nance, about joining the merger. The main concern that stopped Nance was the possibility that he wouldn't be in charge at the new company. Since Nance was considered part of the reason for **Packard**'s decline, the **Nash** and **Hudson** people all wanted the man in charge to be George M. Mason, who had guided **Nash-Kelvinator** through twenty years of profitability.

Packard and Studebaker Merge—and Fade Away—Together

When it was clear to Nance that he would not be the president of the proposed merger, he started talks with **Studebaker**. When **Studebaker** agreed to a merger in 1954 with the **Packard Motor Car Company** with Nance as president, the deal was consummated.

The new company under Nance's leadership was called the **Studebaker-Packard Corporation**. **Studebaker** hoped to gain from **Packard**'s strong cash position while **Packard** would take advantage of **Studebaker**'s

Book-Cadillac Hotel, Detroit, Mich.   10

The Book-Cadillac Hotel in downtown Detroit was a popular meeting place for auto executives. In room 2607, the merger of **Nash** and **Hudson** companies was negotiated. *Author's collection.*

larger dealership network. Unfortunately, **Studebaker** had lost 30 percent of its sales network by 1956.

The plan was that **Packard** would take care of the luxury car market and **Studebaker** would cover the small car market. The joint company also brought out a new in-between model called the Clipper, which was built at the **Packard** plant in Detroit.

Following a disastrous 1956, Nance resigned as president, and the 1957 and 1958 Packards were the last ones of the famous marque. In 1962, **Studebaker** dropped "Packard" from the corporate name, and all production had left Detroit for the **Studebaker** headquarters in South Bend, Indiana. The Packard Plant in Detroit was used temporarily by other companies but then was totally abandoned.

In 1960, the **Studebaker Corporation** began diversifying itself, buying lawnmower, cleaning supply and plastics companies, among others. By 1962, the company was only manufacturing vehicles in its Canadian plant, and by 1966, that plant had closed and **Studebaker** was out of the auto business. Following a 1967 merger with Wagner Electric, and later with the Worthington Corporation, the Studebaker and Packard marques were gone.

Meanwhile, **AMC** soldiered on after George Mason's death in the autumn of 1954. The reins of power passed on to Mason's very capable right-hand man, George Romney, who would later be governor of Michigan. Several years later, his son, Mitt, would become governor of Massachusetts from 2003 to 2007 and the Republican Party presidential candidate for 2012.

New models came out for **Hudson** and **Nash** in 1955 and 1956. Future consolidation with **Packard** was still being considered when **AMC** made a deal to purchase V-8 engines and Ultramatic transmissions in return for **Packard Motor Car Company** making an equal purchase of parts from **AMC**. However, **Packard** didn't keep its end of the agreement and its demise was not long in coming. **Packard** president James Nance still rejected any agreement that had him as anything less than president of any merged companies. Regarding press speculation about George Romney being in charge of a united **AMC** and **Packard Motor Car Company**, Nance referred to Romney as a "neophyte" and said that his job at **Nash** had been "just to hold Mason's briefcase." The anticipated merger never happened.

Romney started **AMC** out on a course of filling the small car niche. By 1957, the Nash and Hudson marques had disappeared, and the company was banking more on the Rambler than any other vehicle. Production was moved to the **Nash** plants in Kenosha, Wisconsin, and El Segundo, California. The first few years after the Hudson and Nash marques were no longer used were difficult for **AMC**, and the company concentrated on the Rambler American. The Rambler Classic and Rambler American marques brought in some good years for **AMC**. By 1964, Romney had ridden the success wave of **AMC** to the governorship of Michigan, and his protégé Roy Abernathy, originally a **Nash** sales executive, took over the **AMC** presidency.

The practice of building small cars began to pay off in 1961 as **AMC**'s Rambler Classic was the number three selling car in the United States. **AMC** cars began to come with options, such as disc brakes, that were not yet available from the Big Three auto companies.

Because the years 1964 through 1967 were slow for **AMC**, Abernathy sold off the Kelvinator appliance division to raise operating capital for the automobile end of the business. The plan worked, as **AMC** went through the 1970s riding a wave of success with its smaller cars, which achieved popularity after the 1973 oil crisis that led to increased gas prices.

The purchase of Jeep from the **Kaiser Company** in 1970 proved to be a milestone in the success of **AMC** for the rest of its history. In 1953, the **Kaiser-Frazer Company** had purchased the Jeep marque from the **Willys-Overland Motor Company** and began manufacturing the popular Jeep, which got its start as a military vehicle. Roy Chapin's son, Roy Chapin Jr., guided the Jeep division to success and, later, was the CEO of **AMC** in 1967.

Near the end of the 1970s, **AMC** continued to release smaller autos, including the AMC Pacer, Matador, Spirit, Concord and Gremlin, with mixed success. The name Hornet, which had been a Hudson brand name, was revived. In 1977, the company had a bad year and entered into a financial agreement with French auto maker **Renault**. During 1978, most of the **AMC** auto divisions lost money, but the company still showed a profit for the year due to strong Jeep sales.

Renault continued to shore up **AMC** in 1979 and 1980 until it owned half of the company. **AMC** introduced a new line, the AMC Eagle, which included reworked, four-wheel-drive versions of the Spirit and Concord lines. The Renault Alliance was a joint venture of **AMC** and Renault in 1983 and was named "Motor Trend Car of the Year." Although the brand initially had good success, distribution problems and dealership repair issues caused Renault Alliance sales to slide, and the last one rolled off the line in 1987.

Renault's president, George Besse, was assassinated on November 17, 1986, in France. Besse had been credited with bringing **Renault** back to profitability but had closed factories and laid off twenty-one thousand workers to do it. In retaliation, the anarchist group Action Directe had a motorcyclist shoot Besse at his home as he emerged from his limo. **Renault** divested itself of its **AMC** stock shortly thereafter, and **Chrysler Corporation** picked it up. The **AMC** line's name was changed to the Eagle line. The still-profitable Jeep continued much as it had before.

9

AFTERMATH

THE GLOBAL AUTO MARKET

The fuel crisis of the 1970s gave the newly reconstituted **Chrysler Corporation** a chance to market smaller, more fuel-efficient cars to the American public. Under leader Lee Iacocca, the company was able to get the jump on **GM** and **Ford**.

As the two largest automakers continued to produce mostly gas-guzzlers, more fuel-efficient Asian and European companies were able to competitively enter the U.S. market. "Buy America" backlash was eased when the **Volkswagen Group** became the first foreign company to produce cars on U.S. soil since the **Rolls-Royce Motor Car Company** manufactured cars in Springfield, Massachusetts, from 1921 to 1931. In 1978, **Volkswagen** of Wolfsburg, Germany, reconstituted a **Chrysler** plant in Westmoreland County of Pennsylvania and began producing Rabbits, Golfs and Jettas until 1987. Soon after, **Volkswagen**, **Toyota** and **Honda** began successfully manufacturing and marketing in the United States and, before long, were providing the Big Three automakers some major competition.

As the NAFTA ruling of the 1990s began to further change the global aspects of marketing autos, many American companies started to outsource their production to Mexico, China and other places where labor prices were cheaper.

As Europe once dominated the auto industry before 1900, after 2000, the balance of power appears to be shifting toward the Asian brands, with the **Toyota Motor Corporation** often topping the American companies in sales.

Since the 2008 recession, the car front in the United States is still headed up by the Big Three, with **Chrysler Corporation** and **Fiat** partnering. The Big Three almost became lost companies themselves when **GM** and **Chrysler Corporation** declared bankruptcy in 2009, with **Ford Motor Company** coming close to it. The top-selling auto companies in the United States now include not only the Big Three but also **Toyota, Honda, Nissan, Volkswagen, Hyundai, BMW, Subaru, Mazda, Audi, Mercedes** and **Kia**. Other foreign auto companies active in the United States are **Jaguar, Alfa Romeo, Lamborghini, Porsche, Land Rover, Maserati, Smart, Maybach, Tesla, Mini, Ferrari, Bentley** and **Rolls-Royce**.

However, even as the U.S. car market constantly changes, the classic cars of the early American years still hold great appeal and are on display to the millions of people who attend the car cruises and visit auto museums in the United States each year.

BIBLIOGRAPHY

Bausch, David K. *Official Price Guide to Automobilia*. New York: House of Collectibles, 1996.

Beck, Lee, and Josh B. Malko. *Auburn & Cord*. Osceola, WI: Motorbooks International Publishers & Wholesalers, 1996.

Butler, Don. *Auburn, Cord, Duesenberg*. Jefferson, NC: McFarland & Company, Inc., 1992.

Einstein, Arthur W. *"Ask the Man Who Owns One": An Illustrated History of Packard Advertising*. Jefferson, NC: McFarland & Company, Inc., 2010.

Foster, Patrick K. *American Motors Corporation*. Minneapolis, MN: MBI Publishing Company, 2013.

Hamper, Ben. *Rivethead: Tales from the Assembly Line*. New York: Warner Books, 1992.

Heaton, Dan. *Forgotten Aviator: The Byron Q. Jones Story*. Boston: Branden Books, 2012.

Hudson Triangle. Ann Arbor: University of Michigan Library, 2010.

Hyde, Charles K. *The Dodge Brothers: The Men, the Motor Cars, and the Legacy*. Detroit: Wayne State University Press, 2005.

————. *Storied Independent Automakers*. Detroit: Wayne State University Press, 2009.

Kimes, Beverly Rae, and Henry Austin Clark Jr. *Standard Catalog of American Cars, 1805–1942*. Iola, WS: Krause Publications, 1985.

Long, J.C. *Roy D. Chapin: The Man Behind the Hudson Motor Car Company*. Detroit: Wayne State University Press, 1945.

Madden, W.C. *Haynes-Apperson and America's First Practical Automobile.* Jefferson, NC: McFarland & Company, Inc., 2003.

May, George S. *A Most Unique Machine: The Michigan Origins of the American Automobile Industry.* Grand Rapids, MI: William B. Eerdmans, 1975.

Olsen, Byron, and Joseph Cabadas. *The American Auto Factory.* St. Paul, MN: Motorbooks, 2002.

Powell, Sinclair. *The Franklin Automobile Company.* Warrendale, PA: Society of Automotive Engineers International, 1999.

Stanley, Richard A. *Custom Built by McFarlan: A History of the Carriage and Automobile Manufacturer 1856–1928.* Jefferson, NC: McFarland & Company, Inc., 2012.

Szudarek, Robert G. *How Detroit Became the Automotive Capital.* Detroit, MI: Typocraft Company, 1996.

Tucker: The Man and His Dream. Directed by Francis F. Coppola. San Francisco, CA: LucasFilm, 1988.

Ward, James A. *Three Men in a Hupp: Around the World by Automobile, 1910–1912.* Palo Alto, CA: Stanford University Press, 2003.

INDEX

ABOUT THE AUTHOR

Alan Naldrett started one of the first used record stores in the nation while an undergraduate at Michigan State. After graduation, he moved to California, where he appeared in documentaries about the San Francisco music scene of the 1980s, booking and playing in New Wave bands. Upon moving to the Fremont area, he became interested in the preservation of the train depot used in the Charlie Chaplin films *The Tramp* and *The Vagabond*. After returning to Michigan in the 1990s, this interest in history expanded to his garnering master's degrees in archival science and information and library science. He then wrote his first book about his home community, Chesterfield Township, and co-authored books on Fraser and New Baltimore. An interest in the hilarious circumstances surrounding the Toledo War led to his book *Forgotten Tales of Michigan's Lower Peninsula*. From there, Alan and his fiancée, Lynn, traveled around the Michigan Thumb area researching his book *Lost Towns of Eastern Michigan*. While learning about the lost settlements of early Detroit, they started investigating the many vacant auto factories in the area. This led to researching the history of the many car companies that once called the Motor City home, and the rest was history, so to speak, as this led to *Lost Car Companies of Detroit*.

CPSIA information can be obtained
at www.ICGtesting.com
Printed in the USA
BVHW04*0757020718
520624BV00012B/441/P